HIRED!

Every Employment Method

Alfred M. Smith

www.theHIREDguy.com

Dave,
Let's hope this is the only time you read this book!
Al Smith
9/9/[illegible]

HIRED!

Every Employment Method

www.theHIREDguy.com

By Alfred M. Smith

www.theHIREDguy.com
ISBN: 978-09997665-0-7

Printed in the United States of America

Editing: Richard Sine
Front cover photograph: Yuri Arcurs; Istock standard license
Front cover design: Kelly Fabian Photography (Atlanta, GA)
Back cover design and portrait: Kelly Fabian
Back cover pictures: Kelly Fabian Photography (Atlanta, GA)

Table of Contents

Chapter 1: *What's wrong with me?*

Not One Damn Thing!

> *But, Al, I have the qualifications...or at least I think I do. I apply out the wazoo to jobs that I'm perfect for, but I hear nothing. My job search is going nowhere. There must be something wrong with me. What is it?*

There's nothing wrong with you or your qualifications. Most likely, you don't know how much job search has changed. What worked before, for the most part, does not work in today's job search world. In short, you don't know *how* to get HIRED!

This book will change all that.

Let's start with what you're doing.

The Evolution of Job Search

You lost your job, got the pink slip, were laid off, redundant, downsized, or right-sized. I got "right-sized" once and wanted to right size their lip. I imagine you felt the same way, even if you quit. Whatever the term, you find yourself seeking employment.

What's the first thing you did? Wait, I'll tell you the things I did: When I got home I yelled at my wife, kicked the dog, and dived into a bottle of booze. Well, that's not quite true, I don't have a dog. All joking aside, I'm willing to bet you did the following:

1. You updated your resume.
2. Found a series of jobs to apply to.
3. Applied and uploaded your new resume.
4. Clicked SEND

5. Then, you waited for the phone to ring, and waited and waited and waited.

Question: Why do we all of us do this?
Answer: It always worked for us before.

Some of us remember when we would take out the classified section of our Sunday newspaper (do you even get a newspaper?), grab a red pencil, find jobs that are perfect for us, craft a cover letter, add it to our professionally prepared resume written on high-quality paper, put a couple stamps on the envelope, march down to the post office, and within two to three days someone with two eyes and a brain would READ your submission. Then came computers.

The job boards (Monster, CareerBuilder and Hotjobs!) came into existence in the 1990s. (Talk about evolution, Hotjobs! has evolved itself out of existence). The aggregators followed (Indeed and Simplyhired, which was purchased by Indeed, and now Google Jobs). If you're going to be on any job board, and you should, I recommend these because if a job is posted anywhere, it will likely be up on the aggregators' database within twenty-four hours. Today, the darling of job search is LinkedIn. This, too, shall pass, especially if the Microsoft-owned LinkedIn continues down its current path of draconian changes. The other major mystery of job search is the dominant use of Applicant Tracking System (ATS) software and Boolean searches where great candidates were neither found nor considered because they don't know how the game is played.

In today's job search world, you can be the greatest candidate available and not even be considered. If you don't have the right words in the right quantity, formatted correctly, your submission likely will not get through, nor will you get found when "they" look for people like you.

Why should I believe what you have to say?

I'm glad you asked

At the beginning of every one of my workshops and keynotes, I recommend participants ask/research that very thing. Should you believe the talking head? Does s/he have something worthwhile to share or will you be wasting your time?

Al's Story:

Let's start with maybe the least important reason: I've been in your shoes. This is personal!

> *I've been at the executive level for many companies in five different industries and have won more awards than I have fingers and toes (I have a full complement of both). But, the last time I found myself in job search mode, it was for more than two years! I was the most miserable SOB who ever walked the face of the earth. Why my wife stayed with me is beyond my ability to comprehend (I'm not making this up).*
>
> *I would apply for jobs anywhere in the country; I'm not married to any city, could be a VP of Sales anywhere, for any company in any industry (a widget is a widget is a still a widget). Crickets, crickets, crickets. I couldn't get a nibble for any of the Vice President of Sales positions for which I was well-qualified. Okay, I figured, I'll take a step back and apply for directors' positions. Nothing. I love training people how to sell CORRECTLY, so I applied for many field management positions. Zip. I couldn't even get an interview for sales jobs.*
>
> *One night, a neighbor (thanks Paul) practically dragged me to a job event at Roswell United Methodist Church (the largest church-based job networking entity in the USA). I had no interest in going (who wants to be around a bunch of unemployed low-lifers?) and had lied to my wife about attending previously. I was amazed. In an assembly hall they served dinner to people who*

looked like me: professionals. There must have been 250 people (a typical turnout). I stood and said, "My God, there's enough good talent in this room to fill a decent-sized company!"

I was so moved by what I experienced I went to its Website the next morning and stumbled onto its prayer request page. Believe me when I say, I am NOT the sort of person who reads other people's prayer requests; I don't go into my wife's purse! But, that day I read four. The last one changed my life.

The guy said, "I've lost my job, I'm virtually penniless, my wife has left me, my house is about to be foreclosed on, and I'm in total despair." I knew exactly what this guy was capable of doing to himself because I had contemplated it too. I swore at that moment…as soon as I got a job, I would help other people get jobs and as part of the employment contract of my next employer, they agreed that every other Monday afternoon I was not working for them, I was volunteering to help people get jobs.

To this day, I volunteer 20% of a normal work week. Volunteering lead me to become a career counselor; which lead to me co-writing my first book, ***HIRED!*** Paths to Employment in the Social Media Era. *Because of this, I have been used as an "expert" (not MY word) newspaper resource, and been interviewed on radio often (I have the face for radio and the voice for silent movies). I'm also a keynote speaker.*

With weekly workshops, averaging about 40+ each week, I have personally assisted more than ten thousand job seekers.

Do I have anything of value to add for you? That's for you decide.

They Hate Your Kind!

We might as well get the most distasteful things out of the way up front. Biases exist.

Ageism (against older workers):
"We are hiring lots of young, vibrant, hungry, and capable analysts."[1]

Ageism (against younger workers):
"[Recent college graduates are] lacking in critical thinking and problem-solving skills (60 percent) and attention to detail (56 percent) as well as writing proficiency (44 percent) and public speaking (39 percent)."[2]

Long-term Unemployed:
"Once you are unemployed over six months, you are considered pretty much unemployable. We assume you were already passed over and no one else wanted you either."[3]

Let's stop there since we are all well aware of other "-isms" against genders, sexual orientations, races, disabilities, etc. Career consultant Amy Lindgren writes, "From my perspective, [hate-isms] spring from baked-in disrespect for entire segments of our workforce. I'm not talking only about women, but about

---

[1] Michael E. Kanell, Metro Jobless Rate Slides on Hiring Push, *The Atlanta-Journal Constitution*, Nov. 27, 2015.

[2] Kelli B. Grant, Hiring Managers Say Many Grads Not Job Ready, CNBC, May 17, 2016.

[3] Cynthia Shapiro, *Corporate Confidential: 50 Secrets Your Company Doesn't Want You to Know—And What to Do About Them (London: Marshall Cavendish Business, 2008).*

laborers, workers with disabilities, those with felonies on their records, people from racial and ethnic minority groups...and yes, white men, when the situation fits."[4]

Okay, it's real for all of us. Time to pull up our "grown-up undies" and get to the work of getting work. Overcoming many biases will be addressed later in the book and the contributing authors and I will help position you to get HIRED!

There's even better news for **YOU**...

Neither the majority of those currently employed, nor the majority of those in job transition, have a clue how drastically job search has changed. This is not to say you're not bright, much less that I'm some genius (I ain't). It's to what the "truths" of job search have evolved. And THIS is to your advantage, since you're reading this book!

Whaddya Got?

You have probably been inundated by claims in books, webinars, and emails that someone has THE way to get a job (If they had invented THE WAY, we would all be using it, right?) You won't get that here and you shouldn't expect some academic or theoretical exercise. This is personal to me – and to YOU!

What I can promise you is every employment method I know and have put into practice in real-life situations. In addition, I have asked over a dozen highly respected specialists to add their insight. There will also be methods I'm not fond of included, but you may find them useful. I don't give a damn how you get a job; I just want you to get a job!

---

[4] Amy Lindgren, Me too, too, too, too, too: sexual harassment at work, *Pioneer Press* (St. Paul, MN), Oct. 22, 2017.

Will this work for me?

It certainly should.

Here are a few success stories:

- A Sr. Financial Analyst in his mid-fifties who had worked for one company his entire career (the original company was bought by a much larger one) was suddenly laid off. He networked like crazy after keyword optimizing his LinkedIn profile and resume. Within a few weeks of launching his "Marketing Campaign," he had 2 job offers to choose between.
- A Solutions Engineer had worked for his family business. The business was in decline and he sought a change. After getting a couple of required certifications, he landed virtually the exact position he desired.
- A third client used a question you will be introduced to in the Interview chapter. The company owner spoke for over 30 minutes. When finished, he said my client was the most brilliant person he'd spoken to in years (the client hadn't said anything)!
- A restaurant manager wanted the promotion he qualified for three years earlier OR another employer. We created a presentation that totally blew away his superiors. He got his promotion, along with a six-figure raise. By the way, his is the #1 group of stores in the national chain.
- A big-box retail district manager needed to move across country where his wife had taken a huge promotion. Once again, we created material that could be presented to both his company and other firms (and was). He received two job offers.
- A Junior Software Engineer graduated from college a year earlier and took "a vacation" for a year. Recruiters wondered what was wrong with him. We positioned his

online profile, so he would be found all the time. Today, the world is his oyster;

- A brilliant Senior Software Engineer attended one of my workshops, talked to me (over my head) and with a fellow volunteer afterward who better understood each other. They argued and argued! Surprisingly to me, he became a client. He described the process as "the toughest homework since college." After uploading his new profile, he received 11 Recruiter views within the first 12 hours! Four weeks and over a dozen interviews (and multiple companies) later, he's HIRED!
- A medical device sales person wanted a new job without his company knowing. Clever wording and inspiring marketing materials helped land his current position.

The methods you will be introduced to have worked for people at every level (staff through C-Suite), all ages (from Millennials to Baby Boomers), and a variety of backgrounds. There are no guarantees, but there's no reason you can't be as successful as my hundreds of successful former clients have been.

My intention is to share the changes in job search protocol, how to improve and add to the methods you currently use, and to introduce you to every method for landing the job you want next. Choose what best fits your personality, but be sure to push your limits! Work on your weaknesses. It will make you a more rounded individual. Besides, you might even find the experience fun.

Finally, I hope to make you laugh (or groan) a bit. I hate most books in this genre; they're as dry as the Mojave Desert. This book is packed with useful information and laced with humor (usually at my expense, there's lots of material). It's intentional.

Job search is one of the worst experiences we go through and you need to laugh. But keep in mind the words of Sir Winston

Churchill, "A joke is a VERY serious thing." My jokes almost always include a serious message.

Think of this:

"Some people look at things
the way they are and ask why.
I dream of things that never were,
and ask why not?"
-Robert F. Kennedy

Why not you? Why not you??? Why not you???

You will get **HIRED!**

It will likely not be as quickly as you want, but it WILL happen!

You will...

Get
HIRED!

Chapter 2: Preparation and Assessments

"Give me six hours to chop down a tree and I will spend the first four sharpening the axe."
-Abraham Lincoln

Turn, Turn, Turn...

The rock group, The Byrds, recorded a song taken from the Bible's Book of Ecclesiastes, *Turn, Turn, Turn.* The first line tells us that there is a *season* for everything. And, unlike what you have been told (and assume to be true), this is NOT the time to write your resume. This is the "season" to till the soil prior to planting the seeds that eventually lead to the harvest season (employment). You will soon be launching a Marketing Campaign; but, as with every marketing campaign, we must start at the beginning. It's time to prepare.

I heard you were wacky, Al, but this is nuts!

You're not the first to say that, but follow this line of thought for a bit. The job search world has changed dramatically. It is process driven. Work the process from the beginning and run into fewer roadblocks.

Before you start tapping away blindly at your new resume and applying into the Black Hole of online submissions, you should gather what you need for success.

Your Cornucopia of Success

You have a lot to offer and will be a valuable asset to your next company, even though you might not think so today.

Losing your job can make you feel worthless and confused about your choices in life. Trust me, I know. You think your life has no purpose. And the longer you're in job transition, the worse it gets. What do you tell people when they ask, "What do you do?"

I haven't worn a watch for over thirty years, but I know if I'm early or late for Church by what's on the radio. I listen to NPR's Sunday Weekend Edition and based on where I am en route when the puzzle is playing lets me know my timing. A few years ago, the host asked the participant, "What do you do?" The person stumbled and fumbled with the answer, finally saying she was unemployed. She couldn't get an answer correct in the game. Listening to that exchange was a painful experience.

In addition to feeling like a leper when in transition, we minimize what we did when we were employed, "Everyone knows I do that" or "That's just a part of the job" or "It's nothing; anyone can do it." Well, no: your next employer will not know you did something unless you state it; it may be part of the job, but unless you say it, s/he will assume you don't have the experience; and what may be second nature to you is something your potential employer has no clue about.

You earned a salary for a reason: you were good at what you did! You have accomplishments, skills, credentials, licenses, and so much more. It's time to reclaim your value!

Like virtually every successful person in sales, I have a "Brag Book." (I have stuff from back in the '70s for God's sake!) You might have one, too, or maybe a portfolio. If so, great! Whether you have this sort of thing already or not, before you get started on your Marketing campaign, you should gather the following:

1. **Old Resumes** - Your previous resumes show your professional history over time. They may remind you of

things you did that you would like to do again (or never do again). They may remind you of a success long forgotten, awards, recognition, training, etc.;

2. **Performance Reviews** - Although currently out of favor, you may have received positive performance reviews from your bosses over the years highlighting elements of your experience that will help you add substance to your personal brand (more about Branding in Chapter 3);
3. **Group or Team Accomplishments** - If you were a member of a team or group at work and that group accomplished or exceeded its goal, you MUST claim that accomplishment as your own. When asked, you can explain that you were a member of a team assigned to do______, the situation was_____, we came up with several potential tactics to accomplish the goal such as _______, the action we chose was________ and the results were ___________. (You just created a S.T.A.R. story (more on that later, too).

A former client had been an editor and/or producer for over twenty years. She'd worked for every news outlet in the Atlanta area, including CNN, but found herself out of work for more than two years. Because of the long jobless period, she had convinced herself she had done nothing of value in her whole career. I told her to write a short professional biography. In it she mentioned she had been a member of a group that had won a regional Emmy some years earlier. I told her, "Freida, you buried the lead!" In Value Proposition decks we created after completing the process you're about to go through, she was branded, "Emmy Award Winner." She got a job quickly thereafter and went to work for a company of HER choice.

4. **Reports** - I have sales reports dating back decades. Data from these can be used to calculate your return on your company's investment in you: your personal ROI. (Note: Be

careful not to share proprietary information. It's not only bad form, it might be a violation of law.);

5. **Work Samples** - Graphics, marketing pieces, pictures, awards, spreadsheets, presentations. Some of these things alone or in combination may become part of your Value Proposition, Value Proposition decks, and Interview Presentations (more about these later);
6. **Publications or Articles** - If you were mentioned in or wrote a work-related article, white paper, or other publication, substance from them can be used to differentiate you from other job seekers. These can help establish you as an industry authority, guru, or specialist;
7. **Recommendations** - You can't get enough recommendations. We can make all the claims we want about ourselves, but when a third party makes a statement about your ability, people are more likely to take notice. More to come later in this chapter about recommendations;
8. **Languages** - Few Americans speak more than one language (some of us don't talk "too good" English!). There's the old joke: *"What do you call someone who speaks multiple languages"* Multi-lingual. *What do you call someone who speaks two languages?* Bi-Lingual. *What do you call someone who speaks only one language?* American." Speaking, writing and/or reading foreign language(s) can set you apart from your competition. Even if you're not fluent, you can claim knowledge, then clarify your level of fluency in an interview;
9. **Associations** - Most professions have an association. There are many local, state, and national associations. Check Weddles.com for an association in your profession. When I checked last, there were about 100 listed;
10. **Accomplishments** - If you're unclear about what is meant by an accomplishment, it's virtually anything quantifiable, such as:
    A. Dollar increases,
    B. Percentages,
    C. Numbers of any kind,

D. Time saved (productivity increase),
E. Before-and-after comparisons

11. **Skills** - Some people think they have no accomplishments; but you got paid for a reason. You have skills such as:
    A. Software skills
    B. Advanced degree
    C. Licenses
    D. Machinery
    E. Specialized and/or formal training
    F. Certificates
12. **Attributes** - Your attributes can be terms (1-3 words) people you have worked with might use to describe you professionally. If stumped, the Missouri State University system is a good resource for ideas:
    www.missouristate.edu/assets/bms/AttributeComp.pdf
13. **College Activities** - Such as:
    A. Institution(s) attended and/or completed
    B. Degree(s) attained
    C. GPA
    D. Clubs
    E. Sports (even intramural)
    F. Greek Societies
    G. Employment during matriculation
    H. Internships
    I. Education abroad
14. **Volunteerism** - Many executives volunteer and the ones who do appreciate others who do, as well. Volunteerism shows you:
    A. Are Civic-minded
    B. Have Character
    C. Had activity during job transition
    D. Are keeping your skills honed
15. **Youth Activities** - Especially if you're fresh out of school with a thin professional background, things you did as a youngster can make a difference to Hiring Managers. These activities could include:
    A. Sports

B. School and other clubs
C. Scouting
D. Farming church or neighborhood activities
E. Academic achievements

Isn't it now obvious just how impressive you become when you include more of your background? Much of this will become part of your Brand, your resume, online profiles, marketing documents, interview material, and your formal Value Proposition.

Recommendations

Generally speaking, Hiring Managers believe job seekers lie through their teeth. That being said, without recommendations, it's virtually impossible to get a job. You can't have too many of them. As much as anything else, a recommendation is a third-party proof source that what you're saying about yourself is true.

The more recommendations you have, the more confident the Hiring Manager will be that you're the right choice among all the available candidates. Recommendations help minimize a Hiring Manager's fear of making a bad hiring decision.

Reconnect with colleagues both current and past, vendors, managers, clients, and others. These are people with whom you have a relationship and who will likely be happy to help you. Who knows, they may even know of a job for you.

Reach out directly. Pick up the phone, make nice. Tell them something about why you enjoyed working with them (they will likely not remember the event, but appreciate that you did. Chances are good they will have a positive story about you).

Explain your employment situation and ask for either a paper or LinkedIn recommendation.

Your chances of getting a well-written note that includes the points you want to make greatly increase if you offer to write the letter for them, "I don't want to put a burden on you, so if your time is tight, I can write the letter, send it to you for approval, and then you can just sign it and send it back in the stamped return envelope I include." You'll get the recommendation sooner, as well. By the way, once you have the letter of recommendation, you have it forever.

LinkedIn's method for requesting (and giving) recommendations is straightforward. Here's LinkedIn's way to make a recommendation request:

1. Go to your LinkedIn Homepage;
2. Click your picture on the top right-hand side;
3. Click View **Profile;**
4. Scroll down to the Recommendation section;
5. Click **Ask for recommendation;**
6. You will see the line: **What do you want to be recommended for?** Click the company of choice from the dropdown box;
7. You will see the line: **Who do you want to ask?** You can choose as many as 3 LinkedIn connections at a time. (I suggest one person at a time.);
8. You will have to **choose your relationship** with the person;
9. The person's position (title) at the time;
10. In the box provided, you can **write the entire recommendation** (We suggest you write it in a Document first, have someone besides you proofread it for spelling and grammar errors, then copy and paste it into the box);
11. Click **Send.**

You can use these recommendations in part or in whole to make points in various marketing documents, such as your Value Proposition deck and Marketing and Interview Brochures. You can claim to be the greatest thing ever born, but if someone else says it about you, there is a greater chance of it being believed.

What do I want to do when I grow up? (Assessments)

Because Recruiters (Talent Acquisition Managers or TAMs) search for talent starting with the job title they are trying to fill, I always ask participants in my workshops to start thinking the way Recruiters work. Instead of asking for an Elevator Pitch, I ask them to state their name and their next job title. Many people say they don't know what they want to do next.

I encourage everyone to consider taking a formal assessment, especially if you're uncertain of your next professional direction. Right now is a perfect opportunity to learn about yourself and what might be the best fit for you. Today's tools can be surprisingly accurate and informative.

Being equipped with clarity about your strengths and weaknesses, what engages and motivates you, your ideal work environment, and the style of manager that best suits you can enable you to make an informed decision. Imagine being excited to wake up and go to a job where you enjoy earning a living. If this sounds good to you, you may want to take a professional assessment.

Many of us have taken assessments throughout our careers. It seems like I have taken a million of them. I can tell you exactly what my DISC and Myers Briggs results will look like, but I always found the assessments I took lacking in substance. Therefore, when a client (Victor) wanted me to listen to information about a new and different assessment, I was skeptical to say the least. Victor had taken and personally paid for the assessment, received a 70-page report, then had a video-type discussion with the administrators. I was impressed. Still, being a natural-born skeptic, I wanted to know more. The principals and I met via video conference where I agreed to take their assessment. This is how I met Steve Graham.

Steve has had a 30-year career as an HR professional in a variety of industries and countries. He is a student of human behavior who has interviewed and hired hundreds of individuals. Having been exposed to most assessment tools available, he now offers formal, professional assessment reviews and will only use tools that have been developed by TTI Success Insights. Steve often says, "TTI Success Insights offers best-in-class assessment tools in over 90 countries. In my opinion, they are more accurate and offer more actionable feedback than any other supplier out there."

> **A**s you continue to prepare yourself in your career search, there are tools that will enable you to differentiate yourself from your competition. Specifically, having a certified specialist interpret the feedback from a TriMetrix DNA assessment is one such tool.
>
> This is both a reliable and valid instrument that combines three distinctly different sciences. The information it delivers will not only offer valuable personal insight, it also provides the clarity and direction to pursue and attain a job or career that will improve your fulfillment both at work and in life.
>
> Let's have a quick look at each science to discover what it tells you:

DISC explains **HOW** you do what you do. It reflects your behavior, how others see you. We tend to adapt our behavior depending on where we are, who we are with, and how we think we should behave at any given time. The end result is to have a successful interaction with one or more people.

One person's behavioral style is not better than another; it is simply different. You can be extremely successful regardless of your style. What you do with your style is what matters most. The DISC assessment offers insight into your style (the role with which you would be most comfortable) and provides actions you can take to flex your style to others to be more effective, as needed. Adjusting your style to another can improve the effectiveness of how you communicate and can be the key to your success as a valued employee.

Driving Forces explain **WHY** you do what you do. They identify your core values. Typically solidified by age 30, Driving Forces are powerful motivators that can engage you into action in both your personal and professional life. Or, they can help you understand what you prefer to avoid. For example, do you care more about gaining knowledge or helping others? Do you work best in a harmonious environment or can you thrive and focus in chaos? This assessment divides your 12 Driving Forces into top four, middle four, and bottom four. The top four, or your Primary Cluster, define what drives your actions. They work together to explain what you are most passionate about. If you are in a role that does not satisfy those passions, you may be disengaged at work.

Competencies are soft skills, or **WHAT** we develop through our work and life experiences. These skills are built over time and become part of your personal talent portfolio. This assessment ranks 25 critical competencies to help you identify which skills you have been recognized for and which may need development. Knowing which competencies you have mastered becomes a selling point when marketing yourself.

Underdeveloped competencies can become goals for future development if they are required for success in the career path you would like to pursue.

As mentioned earlier, you need to assess how you can differentiate yourself from other applicants within the job market. Take direction from the TriMetrix DNA assessment to develop a personal job search action plan. It will help you understand what types of roles, companies, work environments, and managers will best fit your needs. It will also provide you with keywords that you can use to improve how you market yourself through online social media. This tool has helped millions of people around the world for decades.

Contacts

"Six Degrees of Kevin Bacon" claimed we are only a few contacts (degrees) from anyone in the world. You have close friends and relatives, casual and business acquaintances, and ancillary contacts. Each of them have 1st, 2nd, and 3rd level connections, just as you do. In total, you are somehow connected to millions of people, any of whom could hold the key to your next job. Begin assembling a list of 250-300 contacts as a starting point. No, seriously.

Why?

The best stories are the ones we tell on ourselves. Here's one of my, "Al, you need a big dope-slap up the side of your head," stories.

> My wife and I were close to the couple across the street. David and I could often be found telling bad jokes in the middle of the street while our spouses would *girl talk* or do garden work. When I was a pharmaceutical executive, David was the engineer and/or architect at the Georgia Aquarium. They moved to an in-town condo and he eventually became the aquarium's president.
>
> A few years later, we were invited as one of only 14 couples to David and Loraine's 36th wedding anniversary dinner at the Aquarium. Between their move and the party, I had been in job transition...for a LONG time. Since his background and mine were so different, I never thought to let him know my situation.
>
> It didn't dawn on me until I began rubbing elbows with some of the most influential executives of the biggest companies in Atlanta just how stupid I had been. Entre to C-suite executives could have been a couple phone calls away. Have I told you I'm a genius?

Your next Golden Ticket doesn't have to be in the hands of some big wig. You never know who knows whom and is willing to reach out on your behalf. Any contact could be a breakthrough contact!

In the year after Microsoft purchased LinkedIn, dramatic changes were sprung onto its members. Many useful features disappeared, including "Tagging" (being able to note how you met a person, industry, notes, etc.). These tool and others are lost for now, but LinkedIn makes changes like normal people change their socks, so be on the lookout for changes (positive and negative).

Although a real bother, you may want to create a folder on your computer of your LinkedIn contacts by copying and pasting them, so they can be accessed in the event of something dramatic happening to your LinkedIn account. It doesn't happen often, but it can. Here's an example:

> A client (Todd) got locked out of his LinkedIn account. He was contacted by an entity claiming to be LinkedIn Security. He followed the instructions. Access to his account was restored...for 1 day. He called asking for my help. I could see his profile, but he couldn't access it.
>
> I sent a request for help to the LinkedIn tech geniuses on behalf of my client including all Todd's contact information. I received a response telling me (not Todd) that LinkedIn cannot contact him, but the Mensa Candidate writes, "...ask the member to contact us following the below steps.
>
> 1. Click the ME icon at the top of your homepage." (*He can't log into his account, so he can't access his homepage!)*
> There were five additional steps, none of which were possible because Todd couldn't access his account! So, a word to the wise: save everything on a weekly basis. Everything evolves and, though it's the best option for job seekers today, it's possible LinkedIn could evolve itself out of existence.
>
> (Note: 24 hours after my reply to Customer Support's six-point instructions, I received an email from LinkedIn that they finally figured a way to send Todd an email.

Hallelujah!) Thanks to Sindhu of LinkedIn's Customer Support Team for his assistance.

Create a spreadsheet of contacts to replace the Tagging feature no longer offered by LinkedIn. You should categorize your contacts by type of contact (1st level: know well, 2nd level: business or personal acquaintance and 3rd level: New networking contact or some other such category).

If the list becomes too unwieldy, put all your contacts into a set of Excel spreadsheets or other Contact Relationship Manager (CRM), like Hubspot, with sub-categories, including the following information in columns:

- Name
- Address
- Phone Number
- Email
- Company
- Make room for
- Current Date
- Follow-up Date
- Notes

Your list could include friends, relatives, people in your address book, former bosses, colleagues (current and former), classmates, those on your holiday mailing list, LinkedIn Contacts you know, networking event attendees, clients, and vendors. Even include insurance agents, financial analyst, etc. It's in their best interest for you to be employed, right?

You can remove people who don't prove to be valuable, if you so choose.

Bleaching the Red Flags

Since we are being introspective, chances are good Recruiters and Hiring Managers will concoct real or imagined negatives about you as a prospective employee. We affectionately call these Red Flags. Through cold, candid introspection, you can prepare to address those perceived negatives. Many can even be turned into positives. If they are not uncovered and addressed, they will block your chances of getting hired.

Although you may stumble during the interview itself, it's more likely that what they think is a negative will be a misunderstanding of your past or the perception you're lacking a desired trait or ability. No worries, we all have Red Flags! Preparing for them now will ready you for asked (and unasked) questions during interviews. Your answers will just roll off your tongue as if those perceived minuses are advantages.

Let's uncover and address your potential Red Flags:

1. List what you perceive as negatives for someone hiring you;
2. Create a story turning those perceived negatives into a positive OR create a spin minimizing the negative;
3. Formulate questions to uncover possible hidden objections to you so the matter can be addressed with your Red Flag stories;
4. Practice your Red Flag questions and stories until you are comfortable with them and casual in your response.

You should be able to recognize many of your own shortcomings (you're liable to see yourself more negatively than others do), but expand your Red Flag research by asking friends, family, former co-workers and managers for help. Be sure to tell them to pull no punches (and don't take what they say personally!).

Here are some examples of potential Red Flags:

- Education (too much or too little);
- Gaps in your recent professional history;
- "Bridge Jobs" (jobs that don't seem to fit a normal career path - or jobs you took to pay the bills);

- Lack of technical skills, licenses, certifications, etc.;
- Desire to drastically change careers;
- Job history (too many or too few employers);
- Experience (seemingly over or under qualified);
- Age;
- Geographic change;
- Physical restrictions.

How do I overcome Red Flags?

Let's use a resume gap, for example.

Interviewer: Can you explain the gap in your employment history from year X to year Y?

Candidate: Yes, I was caring for an ailing child (or parent), "but those restrictions are no longer a factor and I seek to return to what I do best...

You might explain a Bridge Job by saying, "During the worst recession since the Great Depression, I took that job because I had responsibilities and I didn't want to go on the government dole." Can you see how a statement like this can turn a potential negative into a positive?

Your position may have been eliminated during a downsizing, "...but I can show you glowing recommendations from my former manager."

I often explain that excellent sales people present the positives of their product or service and minimize (or not mention) its negatives. The same stance must be taken in your job search Marketing Campaign. Remember, virtually any Red Flag can be minimized or turned into a positive if you create a plausible story explaining your side of the story.

Planning

In your job and throughout your professional career, you had goals to meet. Job search is no different. You need to set job search goals. Your search plan should include time management, budgeting, financial planning, physical health, and psychological wellbeing.

Plan: Time Management

- **Full time or part time search** - Working at finding work (not just applying into the Black Hole) is a job in itself. Those who put in a full-time effort tend to get hired sooner. Shoot for 30-35 hours per week
  - Start your day early (as you would your normal job)
  - Get the scut work of searching job boards and submitting applications out of the way early
  - Work the time zones - the Continental U.S. has four time zones. If you're in the Eastern Time Zone and it's 5:00 PM, people on the West Coast have three more hours to work.
- **Job Search Activity Quotas**
  - Number of Applications (not just busy work!)
  - Follow-up calls, traditional mail, and emails
  - Proactive and direct contact (Value Proposition decks)
  - Informational Interviews (coffee, lunch, etc.)
  - Networking meetings
  - Job Search events (including job fairs)

I met Eric Handler when I first began my volunteer activity on behalf of those in transition at Atlanta Jobseekers. Eric is managing partner of Handler & Associates and the impetus for JobSeekers.org, a nonprofit that hosts weekly meetings for Atlanta-area job seekers providing practical and spiritual inspiration, encouragement, and search support. He is also the creator of CareerHandler.com, a complete job search system.

Below, Eric shares his suggestions for scheduling 2-weeks out, excerpted from CareerHandler.com

> **A**rguably the most precious resource you have is time. Developing and maintaining the disciplines of planning and managing your time make you feel more in control. Plan your schedule two weeks in advance and block off specific job search time and activities as well as personal time. Here are some examples:
>
> - Identify decision makers from XYZ Company
> - Research new target companies
> - Work on Marketing Plan
> - Work on elevator speech
> - Create networking list
> - Write and send Thank You notes
> - Lunch with spouse
> - Coffee with former employer
> - Respond to emails
> - Search for jobs online
> - Make phone calls to your network
>
> Blocking out two weeks at a time on your calendar helps you ensure that the amount of time you are spending on your job search adds up to the number of hours a week that you planned. This helps you be as productive as possible and remain focused.
>
> The goal is to have your calendar drive your activity, rather than the unplanned less-urgent items. If you were currently employed, you would be clocking in and out. To be successful in managing your time, you should be working on only the items that are listed on your calendar. Be sure to check your calendar at the beginning of each week and at the start of each day.

Planning your activities out two weeks in advance significantly reduces your anxiety level because you always know what you are supposed to be doing and when. It also significantly increases your efficiency.

Choose appropriate times for certain activities:

- During the day
    - Schedule Meetings
    - Make Phone Calls
- During evenings and early mornings
    - Internet search

Remember, if it isn't on the calendar, it won't get done. Schedule all activities in your calendar. Only after you plan your job search calendar, consider carefully allowing yourself or agreeing to do something not on your calendar. Now, plan that two-week calendar!

Plan: Financial Well Being & Budgeting

Financial planning and budgeting are so important, I asked two Financial Planners to offer advice: David Farrell (based in Chicago) and David Frank, (based in Atlanta). They will share their perspectives on these subjects.

David Farrell:

When between jobs, it is important to put a strategy in place that addresses you and your family's financial needs during the transition period. This includes developing a budget, organizing and potentially repositioning your assets, and determining whether to withdraw funds to cover expenses. Because the duration of your job search is unknown, developing a financial transition plan is critical to preserve wealth.

Begin the financial transition plan by creating a budget. List your income and expenses from all sources and break these items down on a monthly basis so that you know what to expect in terms of the timing of cash flows. Income includes spouse's income, severance, unemployment insurance, and investment income, basically any money flowing into the household that can cover expenses. The next step is to prioritize your expenses by ranking them by importance and eliminating expenses that are not essential. Now, you should be able to determine how long your income will cover expenses. Once the income can no longer meet your monthly needs, expenses must either be reduced further or you will need to draw on your assets.

What you will do next is list your assets. Include your emergency fund, bank assets, investment assets, cash value life insurance, annuities, and equity in a property. Rank the accounts and assets by liquidity and look at your overall allocation. You may want to consult a financial professional at this stage. For liquidity, consider how quickly you can raise cash with an account or asset without penalty. Your emergency fund, bank accounts, and non-retirement accounts tend to be more liquid while your retirement accounts, life insurance, annuities, and property tend to be less liquid, although there are exceptions.

Look at your investment portfolio's asset allocation. You want to know how much you have invested in cash, stocks, bonds, and alternative investments (real estate, commodities, unique investment strategies, etc.). Depending on your situation, you may want to consider reducing your portfolio's risk during your transition. Higher risk assets like stocks and commodities tend to be more volatile and you want to avoid withdrawing funds from higher risk assets when prices have fallen. Moving some assets to cash and bonds during this transition period may prove prudent. Be aware of capital gains that you may realize when selling higher-risk assets to move into lower-risk assets.

When you withdraw money from your assets to pay your bills, take funds from your liquid accounts first. Start with the emergency fund and bank accounts. Then work through your non-retirement investment accounts. If you are under age 59½, avoid taking funds from IRAs unless you must. You want to let your investments grow tax deferred as long as possible. If you need to take distributions from a retirement account, the withdrawn funds may be added to your ordinary income for tax purposes and you may be required to pay a penalty tax of 10% on the amount withdrawn. You will want to utilize certain tactics to minimize the tax hit from retirement account withdrawals.

David Frank:

Losing a Job is something most of us have faced. The most important thing to realize is that it is just temporary. It is sometimes easy to lose confidence in yourself or stress about money, but it is important to keep your head high and determine what is most IMPORTANT.
If you have a family, this will certainly be MOST important. Although difficult at times, try not to let your family see your job search or cash flow anxiety, but instead work together to find solutions. This does not mean "bury your head in the sand" and hope you get a job or your money situation miraculously gets better. This means develop a plan for BOTH:

After a Job loss:

A. Review your severance options with your former employer; if you are eligible, take advantage.
B. Are you eligible for unemployment insurance? If so, apply IMMEDIATELY, even if you have a few opportunities already in the works. This process can take time and the sooner you apply, the sooner you will start receiving benefits.
C. Start looking for new employment ASAP. Most people take a few weeks to feel sorry for themselves; these are wasted days. No one is looking out for you or your family except you. You are most marketable when an employer feels they are "stealing you away" from another opportunity.
D. Ask about health care insurance. Are you eligible for COBRA? Is it cheaper to get your own insurance? DO NOT go without health insurance, even temporarily. There are few things that can ruin a financial plan faster than having an unexpected medical emergency.
E. If you have life insurance or disability insurance, please continue these. Your family needs you to make smart decisions regarding these policies.
F. Try not to use your retirement funds to fund everyday expenses over and above absolute NEEDS. Any distributions from 401(k) plans or IRA accounts will be assessed as ordinary income for tax purposes, plus a 10% IRS penalty if not used for an exempt event prior to age 59 1/2.
G. Try not to use credit cards to fill the gap in Expenses vs. Income. Credit card debt can add up quickly, and the long-term effects of credit card debt can be catastrophic.
H. It is important to remember there is no "perfect job." What you don't see on TV is how much time is spent in the film room reviewing film, on the practice court practicing, or in team meetings developing a game plan with coaches. We often see a neighbor or a coworker who we think is making a lot of money and we think they

have the perfect job. Don't wait around for the perfect job while you sacrifice your financial future to do so.

Budgeting:

A. Review all monies coming in: Social Security, unemployment, and severance pay. Add all this together.
B. Review all monies going out: housing, cars, food, insurance, bills, vacations, and camps. Add all this together.
C. Subtract B from A
D. If this number is negative or very close to even: determine needs vs. wants in "B" above
E. Review all wants:
    - A need is something essential, like housing, insurance, or food.
    - A want is something extra like vacations, camps, and babysitters.
    - Food is a need, eating out is a WANT. Try to cut out all "wants" during this work transition period. You will notice that by not eating out, you will be spending less on food and have no need for the babysitter, as well as, the other related expenses.
    - Is it possible to cancel cable TV and just use Hulu or Netflix?
    - Is it possible to sell your expensive car and purchase a cheaper used version or simply go from 2 cars in the household to 1 car and use Uber for the situations where 2 cars are needed?
    - Is it possible to reduce cell phone expenses?

Everyone has expenses they can reduce. Remember, a couple hundred dollars a month can equal thousands of dollars per year in expenses.

Although looking for a job is a temporary situation, the important thing to realize is, "Things are never as bad as they seem." It is important to be mindful not to let this temporary situation spiral out of control with superfluous debt ensuring a short-term situation creates a long-term financial crisis for you or your family.

Psychology of Job Search

Job search can be devastating financially (as noted above), not to mention emotionally. The pressures can cause marriages to end, "unhealthy practices" to emerge and bring on feelings of desperation. I've already told my story of diving head-first into a bottle of booze (and other dalliances that will remain nameless). Suffice it to say, the psychology of job search hits home.

Katherine Seifert, PhD, a psychologist and an expert on mental health, has again agreed to add her clinician's perspective to the effects of job loss on the family dynamic. We hope that her input helps you and your loved ones avoid the pitfalls.

> **A** parent losing a job can affect the entire family. In addition to the financial insecurity, it can cause a change in lifestyle. Stress caused by job loss may lead to conflict among family members. Some may become depressed or anxious. Children may worry something horrific is about to happen from which family members cannot recover. Family members may have headaches and stomach aches that are probably stress-related.
>
> Stress can be a good thing or a bad thing. Good stress can motivate us to work on solving a problem. It's like the amount of effort one needs to pick up a large load. The larger the load, the greater the effort that is needed. However, if the load is too heavy to lift, you can hurt yourself trying to pick it up alone. Too much stress (or bad stress) that overwhelms us for a long period of time can

hurt us, too. That is why family members helping each other makes the load lighter and is essential in this situation.

There are great ways to reduce the stress of job loss on family members. Relax and play together often as a family. Talk about the joys of the family as often as you talk about the hardships. Problem-solve new issues by holding regular family meetings. Say encouraging things to each other. Children need to know that everything, while different, is all right. They need to know that the family will love and help each other in every way possible. However, if a family member has moderate to severe problems with sleeping, eating, mood, concentration, activity level, school, or relationships that lasts more than 2-3 weeks, he or she may need an assessment to see if individual or family therapy is needed.

The number one thing that helps people cope with hard times is support from the people who care about them. It's called social support, and it helps a person put a hardship into perspective, reduce worry, maintain self-esteem, and solve problems. Look for loving things you can do for each other that do not cost money. Families supporting each other through a job loss with encouragement and love can bring a family closer together.

Healthy Habits

Michele Brant is both an Executive Career Coach and a wellness guru. She speaks on both subjects regularly and has graciously agreed to share her ideas with us on effective methods to increase your mental and physical fitness during one of the most trying periods in one's life: job transition.

Putting Wellness First = Optimized Job Search

It's important to maintain your wellness so you can be at your best when looking for your next job. My definition for wellness is, "the quality or state of being healthy in body and mind as the result of deliberate effort." It is an active process where choices are made towards a more optimal existence.

Most of us have heard eating well, regular exercise, and getting enough sleep are important for our health. Did you know they are also important during a job search?
Let's start with the overall benefits:

- **Consistent Energy Levels** - more fuel in the tank to get things done and deal with job search complexities;
- **Resilience** – the capacity to bounce back and keep going
- **Connected Emotions** - able to manage disappointments and less likely to act impulsively.

Eating well

What you eat directly affects the structure and function of your brain and mood. Eating high-quality foods nourishes the brain. Multiple studies have found a correlation between a diet high in refined sugars and impaired brain function — and even a worsening of symptoms of mood disorders, such as depression.

- Stick to whole foods whenever possible;
- Processed foods are addictive and can be harmful to your health with added salt, sugar, and unhealthy oils;
- Easy way to start: increase the amount of fresh fruits and vegetables in your daily diet.

Drinking Water

The human brain is made up of approximately 75% water, so it is no surprise that dehydration has a dramatic effect on brain health.

- Dehydration impacts: mental fatigue, mood changes, premature aging;

- Benefits: supports healthy brain cells, improves blood flow and oxygen to the brain, helps balance mood;
- It's generally accepted you need to consume at least sixty-four ounces of water daily.

Regular Exercise

Exercise changes the brain in ways that protect memory and thinking skills. Indirectly, exercise improves mood and sleep, and reduces stress and anxiety.

- Commit to establishing exercise as a habit;
- Start with a few minutes a day, and increase the amount you exercise by five or 10 minutes every week until you reach your goal

Sleep

Study after study has magnified the importance of sleep to a human's everyday health and function. During a stressful time, it is even more important to remember to make restful sleep a priority so that you can remain focused and positive during your days of networking and job hunting.

- Studies show getting too little sleep may affect your health, mood, and how you think;
- Everyone is different, but most people need 7 to 9 hours of sleep per night;
- It helps to turn off all electronic devices 1 to 2 hours prior to going to bed;
- Sleep loss impairs your ability to pay attention and with decision making.

Other things that are critical but often not addressed are self-care, proper breathing, and taking time for fun.

Self-Care

Self-Care is a very personal thing. It is important to take some time for reflection to determine how you can practice consistent self-care during a job search. As a starting point, take the following assessment. Add questions or dimensions that are important to you. You can use this as a regular check in along the way.

Self-Care Assessment (Check each true statement)

ENVIRONMENT

- Is your office organized so you can find things easily?
- Are your work spaces pile-free?
- Does your home provide you comfort and a peaceful place where you can think?
- Is the temperature in your home and office comfortable?

PHYSICAL HEALTH

- Do you sleep 6-8 hours every day?
- Do you eat fresh, healthful food?
- Do you exercise at least three times a week?
- Do you drink at least five glasses of water each day?
- Do you drink two or less caffeinated drinks per day?

MENTAL HEALTH

- Do you wake up looking forward to your day?
- Do you take the time to acknowledge what you are grateful for?
- Do you arrive at least five minutes early for your appointments?
- Do you take your time when driving?
- Do you have a good belly laugh daily?
- Do you have at least two friends outside of your immediate family who you feel free to talk with about anything?

RELATIONSHIPS

- Do you have people in your life who encourage your dreams?
- Have you said you are sorry to those who feel you have harmed?
- Do you tell your friends/family how much you care about them?
- Have you disconnected from people who repeatedly disappoint, frustrate, or disrespect you?
- Do you have a way of recharging your faith in life?

Tally up the boxes you checked.
TOTAL BOXES CHECKED ______ out of 20 = _______%
Date _____

Set goals to achieve the boxes left blank, one box at a time. Start with the category you scored the highest on so you begin on your strongest foot. Work on this checklist until your score reaches 85% or higher. As your score increases, notice how much your energy increases as well.

Deep Breathing

By breathing deeply, there is a heightened sense of energy and calmness. The mind and body relax, and stress is reduced. Mental alertness is enhanced. To combat stress effectively, we need to activate the body's natural relaxation response. The relaxation response is a physical state of deep rest that changes the physical and emotional responses to stress (e.g., decreases in heart rate, blood pressure, rate of breathing, and muscle tension).

Breathing Exercise

To begin, sit still and tall somewhere comfortable, ideally with your feet flat on the floor. Close your eyes and begin breathing through your nose.

Then, inhale for a count of two ... hold the breath in for a count of one ... exhale gently, counting out for four ... and finish by holding the breath out for a count of one. Keep your breathing even and smooth.

Breathe this way for at least five minutes and you will see a difference in your mood and your alertness.

Taking time for fun

Research suggests that fun and play is good for us. Part of this is due to being in the creative part of our brain when we have fun. When you think in possibilities rather than obstacles, you notice more options and opportunities. Additionally, setting aside time for fun can help you stay optimistic during a long job hunt. Make a list of activities that are enjoyable to you and schedule regular time to do them. Here are some ideas to get you started.

1. Do a physical activity. Get your body moving;
2. Host a potluck dinner based on food themes;
3. Invent a game with a friend. Make up your own rules;
4. Volunteer for a cause that is meaningful to you;
5. Take yourself out on a play date. Go to a museum, craft; store, or paint-your-own-pottery place.

While job search can be a challenging time in someone's life, the stress can be managed and mitigated through careful steps and hard work. Remember to take care of your body. It's the only one you've got. May you have a healthy and positive job search experience!

"Let our advance worrying become advance thinking and planning."
-Sir Winston Churchill

Chapter 3: Personal Branding

"Remember that your reputation is everything. You build your personal brand through everything you do, whether big actions or small decisions, and that brand will stay with you throughout your career."
-Jan Fields

The Person, the Brand

Many people question the notion of branding in job search, but your brand is as important to you as your name. When people speak of you, is it positive or negative? Or, do they ask, "Who?"

The quote above is by the former president of a little business you may have heard of called McDonald's Corporation. In 2012, *Forbes Magazine* named Jan Fields, "one of the most powerful women in business." She says, "Your reputation is everything,"[5] and everything you do positively or negatively affects your perception and, by extension, your career.

You should always be working to enhance your brand (how others perceive you). Your brand should make you recognizable as the best at what you do. It creates demand and makes you valuable.

This isn't just in job search, it can save your job at times. Think of the first thing companies do during a downturn: they reduce headcount. Your brand (reputation) can make the difference between keeping a job or being in search of a new one. But for the time being, let's focus on establishing and/or enhancing what people perceive of you professionally. Let's work on your personal brand.

---

[5] Susan Adams, Seven Ways to Ruin Your Professional Reputation, *Forbes*, Jan. 14, 2014.

Branding in Job Search

To get a job, you need to get in front of people who have jobs to fill. I think they call those things interviews. But when you apply into the Black Hole (like everyone else) how can your application be different from any of the others? I suggest differentiating yourself through "Personal Branding."

Branding yourself is like a marketing team branding any other product. What is it about the product (you) that can separate you from the other products on the grocery shelf (other candidates)? Does the brand's name, logo, jingle, history, and/or advertising speak to a recognizable value for the potential buyers (the Hiring Manager, next employer)? Branding efforts need to be coordinated.

One of my favorite branding (re-branding) stories is about a horribly-named product called Dow Bathroom Cleaner. The Johnson Wax people bought many consumer brands from Dow Chemical Company, including Dow Bathroom Cleaner. For obvious reasons, S. C. Johnson needed to change the name of the product. Why promote another company with your ad dollars, right?

Somebody at S. C. Johnson recognized the product's brand had nothing to do with the product name itself; as a matter of fact, the name Dow Bathroom Cleaner is self-limiting. Why couldn't a bathroom cleaner not work in a kitchen? The product's advertising slogan vividly and visually spoke as the brand. Scrubbing Bubbles was then fully integrated as both product name and slogan. (I'm going to play the commercial in my head all night now.)

Branding = Differentiation

Entrepreneur, the Small Business Dictionary, defines branding as, "The marketing practice of creating a name, symbol or design that identifies and differentiates a product from other products." Let's adapt that to you and your job search.

Your goal: Create a name, symbol, or sign that differentiates you.

Increasingly, I have become known as "The HIRED guy." This is my brand, in part because of the title of my books and, I hope, because I've gained a reputation for helping people get HIRED! My buddy, Dan Jourdan, is a motivational speaker and sales trainer, "the Sales Energizer." If you have the pleasure of attending one of his events, you will understand the Energizer part. I keep waiting for a rabbit beating a drum to march across the stage.

Your brand doesn't have to be as "in your face" as mine or Dan's. It can be subtle like a black-on-white person carrying a briefcase if you're a salesperson, it could be a woman behind a desk for an administrative assistant, Caduceus (medical symbol), the Scales of Justice, it could be a person with numbers in a thought bubble, line graph, or even a word cloud of terms used in your profession.

Why would I want to use something like that?

Remember the adage of a picture being worth a thousand words? Images (like the Scrubbing Bubbles) can stick in one's mind.

Where would I use them?

You will use them throughout your Marketing Campaign on:

- Business Cards,
- Marketing Brochures,

- Value Proposition deck,
- Email Signature,
- Stationary or memo pads.

An adaptation of The American Marketing Association's definition of a brand can be used to fully formulate your Brand so you are seen as the only candidate who can provide a solution for their need(s).

All good Brands:
1. Confirm your credibility – Show this through your accomplishments, professional history, references, assessments, and other credentials;
2. Understand and satisfy the wants and needs of your targets (employers) – Research the needs of companies seeking people with your job title and state attributes satisfying those needs (see the keywords from job descriptions);
3. Deliver your message in clear, understandable terms – Through the use of a Value Proposition deck, Marketing Plans, Marketing Brochures, your resume, and online profiles;
4. Connect to your Target companies emotionally – Use S.T.A.R. stories used to answer questions in interviews;
5. Motivate the Hiring Manager to a decision – Make a "blow them away" impression by using an Interview Brochure and/or Value Proposition deck.

You don't need to "sell" yourself. Do you know *anyone* who wants to be sold? I bet the answer is no. Present yourself by allowing your brand to show them who you are and what you bring to the table for THEM so they want to make a buying decision. Being authentic is much more appealing than being seen as a used car salesman so don't be overly or overtly self-promoting.

Remember, your brand is the value people see in you, in what you represent, in what you bring to the table for THEM. Show how you can satisfy their needs, how you take care of their pain points. Be upfront and honest. Don't try to be something you're not! How you present yourself is important, but it's not the end-all-be-all. Think "stuff, not fluff."

Remember everything you uncovered about yourself in the previous chapter. You're more impressive than you thought, right? Let's take out the Shinola and shine up your brand so employers will see you for the outstanding addition you will be for them.

Story Time

In almost all cases, answering questions in the form of stories (real-life examples) is superior to merely answering questions with short phrases. There's a balancing act though, because most of us are poor storytellers. It's either Dragnet's Sgt. Joe Friday, "Just the facts, ma'am," or "First I slithered from the primordial ooze, grew legs and lungs then walked fully erect." Yawn!

Don't you love the snappy, one-line comebacks in comedies? Much time is spent in their creation, presentation and timing. Putting together good stories is an art that needs to be learned and then practiced towards perfection.

Fortunately, there are many typical (dumb) interview questions you can anticipate and prepare stories for well in advance. Some include:

- Tell me about yourself.
- Where do you see yourself in 5 years?
- What's your greatest weakness (strength)?
- Why are you interested in working for us?
- Why did you leave your last position (Why are you seeking a new position?)?
- Don't you see yourself as over/under-qualified?
- Tell me about your worst manager.
- Do you have any questions?

Other questions you should prepare in advance for include:

- Give me an example when you had a disagreement with a supervisor/subordinate and how you handled it.
- Give me an example of how you ________ (about an accomplishment or other claim.

Starting with your Red Flags. Write down the perceived problem on the left side of a two-column document. On the other side, write everything about it. Now comes the "fun part." Try exchanging negative words with positive ones. Minimize what you might be lacking by adding, but I have______ which is similar. "Although I don't have that specific experience, I have worked in similar situations. In fact...." Then go on to lay out your STAR story that features something positive.

If you did something untoward, and they're aware of it or ask about it, it's best to admit to the offense then explain the situation from your perspective and what you learned from the experience. "Why did you leave your last job?" might be one of those hard-to-answer questions.

When you have a draft completed, you need to distill the verbiage into a shorter version then a shorter version still. Think Hemingway, not Faulkner! Get to the point; short stories, not novels.

Remember the K.I.S.S. system, "Keep it Simple Stupid!"
The next part of creating stories to practice, practice, practice. Record yourself. Ask the question or concern aloud, pause for a moment, then tell your story. Listen carefully to the replay and work on areas of weakness (and strength) until the story flows. Don't forget, the interviewer puts their britches on the same way as you, so speak as if you're talking to an equal (you are).

Dyslexia: STAR v. RATS

STAR stories have been around for as long as I can remember. There are a bunch of different names for STAR stories such as SAR. I don't know what the hell a SAR is, but I can visualize STARs, can't you? Besides, without the "T" portion, it always seemed to me that not much thought or additional input was given.

Every time I find myself going off on some tangent (like now), I try to focus on the elements of STAR stories to refocus. The elements of STAR are the basis from which every story (not just in job search) and professional presentation should be formed. The acronym STAR stands for:
S-SITUATION or the basis of the event;
T-TACTICS or tasks that were under consideration;
A-ACTION chosen to accomplish the goal;
R-RESULT of the action taken.

Every STAR story should be both compelling and concise. They will help you paint a practical and emotional picture for Hiring Managers (and others you present to after you GET HIRED!). It should be the foundation on which you build all your stories (STAR, RATS and Red Flag).

What do you mean by rats? Yuck!

I mentioned my buddy Charlie Brown earlier (believe it or not, he lives in a town called Woodstock - the little bird in the Charlie Brown comics - and has a cat named Snoopy). Charlie reminded me that not all Hiring Managers want to listen to the entire STAR story, some only want the results when they ask a question. Good point, Charlie!

In one of my workshops, I address this scenario with the question a Hiring Manager might ask:

"Can you give me an example of a change you made that positively affected your company?"

You have the option of diving into a STAR story or just answering the question. If the interviewer only wants the facts, you could use a R.A.T.S. story something like:

"Um, as a matter of fact, I can. I once helped save the company 1.5 man-hours per employee per day through the implementation of an efficiency program. Savings for my group was in excess of $300,000 on an annual basis."

If they want to know more, dive into you STAR story. In the workshop, this is the response:

"There was a corporate-wide efficiency push **(Situation)**.

So, my group got together and came up with the idea of either providing each employee with a separate set of tools or moving tool cabinets out from their present cages in the back of the shop **(Tactics)**.

We concluded that although separate tools was the most efficient method, it was too costly an option. With moving them to pods within a couple steps of where they were used was the best option **(Action)**.

The net result was a dramatic increase in efficiency to the tune of in excess of $300 grand without any additional expense. Similar programs were instituted nationally **(Results)**.

Try reading this STAR story aloud and time it. It takes about 40 seconds. You should shoot for all your STAR stories to last 30 seconds on the short side with a maximum of 60 seconds.

This is an example of a "Situational Interview" question. Companies like to ask situational questions because they see them as a good predictor of your future behavior as their employee.

Note: If they don't want to hear more, forget trying to get the job and start having fun with the interviewer. I say this only a little tongue-in-cheek, as you'll find out in the Interview chapter.

As I said in the previous subchapter, work on the content of your stories. Take out the superfluous information, distill it to a workable story. Practice the recitation in front of a recording device (including video). Listen to what you say and how you say it. Does it sound conversational or forced? Then ask yourself, "Would you buy this story?"

Lehigh University's Career Services web page is a great resource for STAR stories.[6]

Elevator Speech or Elevator Pitch?

Everyone seems to preach the same gospel about the necessity of having an Elevator Speech. I disagree. Most elevator speeches I've heard are a cure for insomnia. They last as long as it takes to get to the top of the Empire State Building ... from your house! We live in a Twitter world of short attention spans. Get to the point already!

Besides, you don't want a speech, you want a pitch.

---

[6] Lehigh University, The Center for Career & Professional Development, *How to Prepare for a Behavioral Interview.*

Think baseball. It's 60 feet six inches from the pitcher's rubber to home plate. Just as with your STAR stories, an elevator pitch should be completed in 30 to 60 seconds.

A traditional elevator pitch should include:

- Your name,
- What you do (be specific),
- What you bring to the table for your next company,
- Your value proposition.

Many pundits will tell you to include a list of 3-5 target companies, but whenever I've had to endure elevator speeches, I tend to hear the same laundry list of mega corporations. This is another mistake, in my view.

Better than stating a list of companies would be to explain what you do for companies, where you would fit (what you bring to the table). Remember, though, don't get too deep in the weeds with technicalities. Most people won't understand.

Don't try to be all things to all people, either. How many times have I heard, "I want to keep my options open." What happens when you try to be everything to everybody, you become nothing to nobody! People should be able to "see you" in a position. Although counterintuitive, the more specific you are in your goals, the easier it is for you to be seen as a fit. This certainly is the case for both Recruiters and Hiring Managers.

If you have worked for any length of time, you've probably been assigned many tasks and your experience has evolved. In short, you've worn many hats. This can be a problem when crafting your resume, online profiles, and elevator pitch. The more you can focus on what you want to do next, the better off you are.

Networking guru Eric West touts a 10-second elevator pitch (I'm liking this already) that contains three elements:

1. Your name,

2. What you do, and
3. One company you want to focus on.

No matter the length of your elevator pitch, and just as with your STAR and Red Flag stories, a successful elevator pitch flows as if it's second nature. To accomplish this goal, I suggest you do 3 things well in advance of your first effort:

1. **Write it** – to include all the essential stuff and remove the unnecessary fluff;
2. **Rehearse it** – so it flows naturally;
3. **Recite it** – to everyone as often as possible.

If you want a more traditional elevator pitch, Nancy Collamer's article in *Forbes*, "The Perfect Elevator Pitch to Land a Job,"[7] is a good place to start. Although the title is an over-the-top exaggeration, the content is terrific.

Can you tell I'm not a big fan of an elevator pitch?

The best advice I've found regarding elevator pitches is by Sam Horn, "When asked *What do you do?* Never TELL them." She explains, people should turn the monologue into a dialogue by involving the other person. Have them make an emotional connection so they can see what you do (Isn't that what I've have been preaching all along?). Here's an exchange Ms. Horn had with someone trying to explain what he did for a living and how he could be more successful:

> **Horn**: "What are the *end results* of what you do that we can see, smell, taste and touch?"
> **Candidate:** He thought about it for a moment and said something about credit cards, online purchases, financial software and computers.

---

[7] Nancy Collamer, The Perfect Elevator Pitch to Land a Job, Forbes, Feb. 4, 2013.

Horn: "Do you make the software that makes it safe for us to buy stuff online?"
Candidate: "Yes! That's exactly what I do."
Horn: "That's good ... but don't *tell* people that."
Candidate: "Why not?"

Horn: "Because if you *tell* people, 'I make the software that makes it safe for you to buy things online, they'll go, 'Oh,' and that'll be the end of the conversation. You don't want to *close* the conversation; you want to *create* a conversation."
Candidate: "So what do I do instead?"

Horn: "*Ask*, 'Have you, a friend or a family member ever bought anything online ... like on eBay, Travelocity or Amazon?'" You just increased the odds they've *experienced* what you do or know someone who has. They may say, "Well, I never shop online. But my wife's on Amazon all the time. She loves the free shipping." Now, confirm your connection by linking what you do to *what they just said*, "Well, our company makes the software that makes it safe for your wife to buy things on Amazon."[8]

I can't think of a better way to explain what you do and what you want, can you?

"All of us need to understand
the importance of branding.
We are CEOs of our own companies: Me Inc.
To be in business today,
our most important job is to be

---

[8] Sam Horn, Why NEVER Again Give an Elevator Speech, LinkedIn, Oct. 7, 2015.

head marketer for
the brand called You."
-Tom Peters

Chapter 4: Targeting

"There are lots of jobs in search of talent. And there's lots of talent in search of meaningful work."
-Maynard Webb

Could this be you?

In his *New York Times* article, Michael Winerip told the story of a Baby Boomer with an MBA who worked as a buyer for a major grocery chain. With a six-figure salary, he was no bag boy. At 56, he got the axe.[9]

Ten months into his search, he had applied to 400 job postings, had a heart attack (without health insurance), and was forced to move his family into his mother's basement.

Some relatively bright guy named Albert Einstein concluded that doing the same thing repeatedly while expecting different results is the definition of insanity. He may have something there.

Bows and Arrows

We greatly improve our chances of hitting a target if we aim in its direction. In a similar vein, you want a job so you go to where you *think* the jobs are: Job Boards and Company Career Pages. Yet, if the numbers cited about the Hidden Job Market are remotely accurate, you're firing in the wrong direction. What was that line about the definition of insanity again?

Applying to posted jobs willy-nilly can mostly be defined as busy work. Avoid this habit and quit eating the same old soup of

[9] Michael Winerip, Setback by Recession, and Shut out of Rebound, New York Times, Aug. 23, 2013.

"targeting" only posted job. Real targeting takes discipline, research and networking.

Now, I'm not so naive as to believe you won't continue to apply to posted jobs even though it's reported, "... you have a 1.2% chance of getting a job through an online application."[10] I gave up attempting to slay that dragon years ago. But can we agree you'll limit the time you spend on job boards to a couple hours first thing in the morning or late at night? If so, you can then spend the rest of the day targeting specific companies, industries, and people to begin the networking that works.

Targeting and Networking?

For years, CareerXroads has claimed about 75% of all jobs are landed through networking. Along the same lines, Lou Adler recently conducted an unscientific study with 3,000 respondents, concluding 85% of jobs are found through some form of networking.[11]

I'm not talking about the kind of networking where you sit around a table with seven other people, also unemployed, looking for the exact job as you. If someone can explain how that one's supposed to help you get a job, I'm all ears! No, I'm talking about a different kind of networking. Wouldn't it make more sense to target companies you want to work for, find people inside these companies and somehow network our way into the companies to put yourself in front of the people who can hire you?

***Targeting* - Industries**

---

[10] Michael Winerip, Setback by Recession, and Shut out of Rebound, *New York Times*, Aug., 23, 2013.

[11] Lou Adler, New Survey reveals 85% of all Jobs are Filled Via Networking, LinkedIn, Feb. 29, 2016.

If you are established in an industry, and want to stay in it, your industry targeting is a straightforward endeavor. Just be certain that your industry of choice hasn't gone the way of the landline telephone.

What industry or industries would you choose to work in? Are there industries you want to exclude?

I have a varied background, having been an executive with seven companies and worked in five industries. My background is sales (sales, sales management, sales training, and executive-level sales and marketing). To me, a widget is a widget. The principals are the same across industries. Although this is common sense, too many Hiring Authorities and Recruiters can't see that one's skills transfer across many industries.

You may have to overcome the challenge of the simpletons who want, prefer, or require only industry-specific candidates. (We'll discuss methods for getting around and getting through these ostriches using social media positioning and marketing materials such as Value Proposition decks and/or interview presentation tools.

For now, just choose a couple industries you would prefer to work in and we can move onto targeting companies.

Targeting - **Companies**

Wouldn't it be a novel idea to work for a company for which you want to work? There's no worse fate than dreading every moment at work, the culture, your boss, or the company itself. You can pick up a lot about a company's culture from its website, especially its Homepage. You may want to look for diversity of sexes, races, ages, etc.

Search your target companies' employees on LinkedIn. If all you see are youngsters and you have had a "Clairol Moment" or two, chances are good you won't fit their culture. On the other hand, if you are fresh out of college and all you see are "Grecian Geezers," you may want to look elsewhere.

Try connecting with a few former employees of a target company via LinkedIn for the low-down on the company's culture, reputation, and style of management. There's no law against asking former employees their opinion of the company or their reason(s) for leaving. Glassdoor is another resource to consider. If you're in the pharmaceutical industry, however, I would steer clear of Cafepharma because it appears to be a place for disgruntled employees and former employees to gripe anonymously.

Hoovers.com and ZoomInfo.com are other resources for in-depth information about companies you know. They are also great ways to uncover companies you were unaware of. I recommend you NOT use these tools from your home computer because they will try to get you to subscribe. You already are a "Subscriber"; you pay taxes. My suggestion is to use your public library. Many (not all) counties, parishes, and provinces subscribe.

LinkedIn and job boards are also good sources for targeting companies. You can conduct a national search for companies seeking to fill positions with your job title. It's easy by clicking on a link to their home page.

Finally, an Executive Resume Writer (who asked for anonymity because her article was for LinkedIn Premium) suggested the following six steps for putting together a target list of companies:

1. Look at industry peers;
2. Consider vendors and clients of previous employers;
3. Check out "Best-Of" lists;
4. Perform a geographical search (of companies);
5. Pursue companies that fuel your passions and match your hobbies;
6. Seek out like-minded coworkers who share your Interests.

Please aim for a list of about 200 companies nationally or even globally. You can prioritize them in any manner you see fit, but don't reach out to the best on the list at the start of your search. More on that in just a bit.

Targeting - Executives

After you have a list of companies you want to work for, it's time to research their executives. What will be your next title? You can use LinkedIn, the *Wall Street Journal*, Hoovers, ZoomInfo, Google Alerts, and other sources to uncover many public and private company executives.

Seek names and background information for everyone from the company president and CEO to the person to whom you will report. The closer you get to the final interview stage, the more valuable this research will become. As you launch your Marketing Campaign, though, these executives can be targets for some of the marketing devices you will be introduced to later in the book.

I can't contact executives!

Oh, yeah? Why not? Don't executives put their britches on the same way as you? And if you send something impressive enough, don't you think it's possible for an executive to instruct those below him/her to talk to you? *"This person is pretty impressive, I want you to set up an interview."* Remember, smart executives want the best and brightest because they, unlike many mid-managers, know surrounding oneself with great talent makes everyone look better. Besides, what's the worst that can happen? You can't get fired for a job you ain't yet got!

One last thing about the habits of executives: They tend to keep a file full of people who, at some point, impressed them. It may take years, but I have a long list of stories about getting a call out of the blue from executives. You never know what will impress someone. Give it a try. It can't hurt.

Targeting - Scum Buckets

You need to include a list of about five companies that you wouldn't be caught dead working for.

Are you crazy or smokin' some whacky tobacky?

I never liked smoking what you're suggesting, and this won't be the last time you question my sanity, but hear me out. There's method to my madness. Not only do I want you to have a handful of scum bucket companies in your target list, I want you to go after them first.

Why?

Practice. There's an old saying in the theater, *"Take the play to Poughkeepsie before you bring it to Broadway."* You're going to make interview mistakes. Wouldn't you rather make them with Pond Scum companies than with one of your key targets?

If you can "fog a mirror" when you breathe, you will get approached by insurance and financial services companies, if you haven't already. A while back, a coaching client announced he had an interview upcoming with one of the worst of those companies. First, I screamed, "No!" then said, "I take that back. Go on the interview for practice, but don't even THINK about taking the job they will offer...and they will make you an offer."

Please trust me when I say you do not want to take a job with a Scum Bucket company. Your genius author made this mistake once and I want you to avoid what I experienced:

> I co-created the first, last, and only manufacturer's rep. sales company in the pharmaceutical industry. We were

so good at what we did, four major contracting companies took their product(s) back and created their own, in-house sales forces. Although I'd made a pretty penny, it was nowhere near enough for retirement; besides, I was way too young to retire.

I received a call from the Vice President of Human Resources of a pharmaceutical company with one of the worst reputations in the industry. It was looking for a Vice President of Sales and Marketing. Even though I didn't expect it to go anywhere, I accepted the invitation for an interview, flew to Newark, and drove to its office.

Interviews were with several people, starting and ending with the President and CEO. And when I tell you the Charm Offensive was on, I mean it was on. "We know we need to change our management style and you're the person who we think can do it."

Every candidate needs to have three salary numbers: A "walk away number" where you can't accept a salary that low, a dream-only figure or "Pie in the Sky number," and a "Goldilocks range" (more about this later in the book). In this case, I was offered $40 grand above my pie-in-the-sky number. How could I say no?

Woulda, coulda, shoulda.

Not long after starting, I got another call from the Vice President of Human Resources telling me that my management style was different from theirs and I was fired. Of course, that's not the real reason I was let go. Part of what the company needed was better marketing material. Therefore, I set about creating outlines for the marketing people to follow, but I wanted the clinical studies behind our claims. There were none! Whew, I dodged a bullet there!

By creating a thorough target list of industries, companies, and executives, you will be able to aim your Marketing Campaign better than those firing in every direction. Now, let's put your list to work.

Networking

Developing an extensive network of contacts has never been as important as it is in today's job search environment. It may even be the most important aspect of your job search. Unfortunately, for many of us, it will force us to do the uncomfortable: put down the devices and have human interaction.

Meaningful, face-to-face conversations make you human. Networking with individuals is a way to ask questions (then listen to the answers!), to gather information, and for others to see you as something other than another piece of paper in the queue of resumes.

Attend business conferences; go out of your way to speak to people; and follow up meeting someone by sending a note, email, Marketing Plan, Value Proposition deck, and request to connect. It's amazing how seldom smart people institute these simple, common-sense methods.

With few exceptions, I speak every Monday of the year leading job search workshops. I take an attendance log and send out one email for giving the participants the opportunity to expand their network. My plea is for them to connect with their fellow participants and me (I hate spam and don't solicit business through these emails). Only about 10% reach out to connect. By the way, if you want to connect, feel free to reach out to me via LinkedIn; my address is: alsmithHIRED.

The Atlanta area, especially its northern suburbs, has the highest concentration of church-based job networking events in the country. You can literally attend one every day of the week. Many are of value; but, as I said before, sitting around a table of unemployed people looking for the same job makes no sense. Instead, I believe you should surround yourself with people who have jobs ... they likely know about more jobs than those who don't have one.

CareerXroads is a membership community of TAMs that claims 75% of all jobs are filled through either employee referrals, the personal network of Hiring Managers, or recruiting via social media.[12] Let's review these methods of networking:

- **Employee Referrals:** It's long been a truism that the best way to get a job is to be referred to the Hiring Manager by a well-thought-of employee. That recommendation, along with your resume, can go directly from your connection to the Hiring Manager.

I recommend seeking an insider who can champion your cause for posted jobs, hidden jobs, or introductions to executives. More often than not, this is a net positive.

Most companies promote employee referrals. It can be a tremendous savings for companies because the cost to hire a new employee can range from $4,000 to $18,000. They feel the referral is legitimate and that the employee has the best interest of the company at heart. Companies have also found both the quality of the candidates and their retention rate is greater with internally referred candidates. Because it's so helpful, many companies offer employees a referral fee.

In his *New York Times* article, "In Hiring, A Friend in Need Is a Prospect, Indeed," Nelson D. Schwartz states that employers

---

[12] Nelson D. Schwartz, In Hiring, a Friend in Need is a Prospect Indeed, *New York Times*, Jan. 27, 2013.

increasingly rely on current employees to refer new hires to bypass endless applications from job-search sites.

Companies seek to increase employee referrals in their overall acquisition process because Applicant Tracking System (ATS) software packages are far from perfect. Schwartz cites the accounting firm Ernst & Young as having internal referral hiring goals. "As a result, employee recommendations now account for 45 percent of non-entry-level placements at the firm, up from 28 percent in 2010."[13] Direct referrals are often seen as an excellent way to minimize the risk of making a bad choice, especially when Hiring Managers can lose their job for making bad hiring decisions.

In her aptly titled, Recruiter.com article, Sarah Duke lays out 10 employee referral program fast facts. Referred candidates[14]:

1. Retention rates are 46% vs. 33% from other sources;
2. Finish training and onboarding almost 50% sooner;
3. One-third of companies plan referral program implementation;
4. Are three to four times more likely to be hired;
5. Forty-one percent of referrals are from the external network of companies (remember the manila folders I told you managers all keep?);
6. Produce 25% more profit than hires from other sources;
7. Referral programs save companies $3,000 or more per hire;
8. Sixty-nine percent of companies' referral programs offer employees between $1,000 and $5,000 cash incentives;
9. 15% offer paid time off or additional vacation days as an incentive;
10. Seventy-five percent of companies use automated referral program systems to manage their programs;

---

[13] Nelson D. Schwartz, In Hiring, a Friend in Need is a Prospect Indeed, *New York Times*, Jan. 27, 2013.

[14] Sarah Duke, 10 Referral Program Fast Facts, *Recruiter*, Mar. 31, 2015.

Are you getting excited yet?

Any of your contacts could be insiders or those who can put you in contact with insiders. Mine your contacts thoroughly. In fact, you will be asked to contact and follow up with all these folks on a regular basis. And don't forget to troll companies and groups through LinkedIn for people to connect with.

The referrals you seek are from employees of your competitors, vendors, former colleagues, and clients. They may have inside information and connections at their current or former employers.

- **Hiring Managers' Personal Networks**: Virtually every Hiring Manager keeps a file of people whom the manager would be interested in hiring. Often, being in a Hiring Manager's personal network enables those candidates to learn about an upcoming job before anyone else. Additionally, Hiring Managers and executives have been known to add qualifications to a job description that only the preferred candidate possesses. They can also have a job posted just long enough for their candidate of choice to begin the application. The job is then taken down within minutes of it having been posted. (No joke!)

There is no "Job Search Fairy." Few of the executives you contact will have a job for you at the moment you make contact. Don't give up! If you become a member of the "inner circle," you may find yourself hired for a dream or other hidden job.

Keep normal turnover in mind. According to a Society for Human Resource Management (SHRM) 2012-2013 report, overall corporate turnover for all industries averages 15%

annually.[15] – Another reason to stay in contact with your network!

Remember, executives change jobs, too. When they land, they tend to surround themselves with people from their personal network. John Zappe of Execunet, a company that helps senior-level executives find new opportunities, reported the average executive's tenure in any position declined between 2005 and 2008 to a scant 2.3 years, a 15% drop.[16]

- **Social Media Recruiting**: LinkedIn is a Recruiter's primary search tool. This is where the largest percentage of the hidden job market lies. Recruiters can often find enough qualified candidates to fill any job within minutes. When they have accrued sufficient numbers, the scouting ends. Their number is usually no more than 25 individuals for any job requisition; therefore, if you're not positioned on the first couple pages of results, you never get a call no matter how qualified you are. Keywords are so important in today's job search universe that I devoted an entire chapter to them!

"And those that were seen dancing were thought insane by those who could not hear the music."
-Friedrich Nietzsche

---

[15] Terrie Nolinske PhD., Survey Research Yields Data on Employee turnover, National Business Research Institute.
[16] John Zappe, Survey Says Executive Tenure Shortening, *ERE Recruiting Intelligence*, May 28, 2009.

Chapter 5: Keywords & Boolean Searches

"It brings up happy old days
when I was only a farmer
and not an agriculturist"
-O. Henry

What's in a Word?

Shakespeare wrote, "A rose by any other name would smell as sweet," which may be correct in literature. But when searching for a job, it's more like what Alan Swan, in the movie *My Favorite Year,* said, "A rose by any other name would wither and die!"

Al, you're nuts!

You've told me that before, but who's counting? Let me give you a couple examples of what I mean:

Many years ago, as a hot-shot sales person, I sold more of a few types of "Medical Capital Equipment" than anyone in the country, but if I wanted to go back to do the same thing, no one would ever find me because there is no longer any such thing as medical capital equipment. It's known as DME, Durable Medical Equipment. They mean the same thing, but I would have to translate what I did to what it's called today.

Here's a similar story:

A Senior Financial Analyst who had worked for the same company all his life (his initial company was bought by the market leader), but suddenly found himself out of a job. He had great qualifications, but his job search was on the rocks. He became a client and went through the "Words-to-Work" process to discover the keywords for his job title (coming later in this chapter). Within five weeks of adjusting his LinkedIn profile and resume, plus aggressively networking, he had two job offers in hand.

If you want to get HIRED in the current job search world, both the quality and quantity of the words you use are a critical element that cannot be overstated. Let's make certain you don't *wither and die.*

The Hidden Job Market

For decades, it's been widely reported that the clear majority of jobs in America are never posted. Just for argument's sake, let's assume 82%-85% of all jobs are hidden, as has been reported in *CNNMoney*, and, more recently, *Forbes*. In the most amazing statistic I discovered while conducting research for my original book, *Millennial Branding* (in a 2012 article) showed candidates are spending time applying in direct opposite proportion to where the jobs are.

Baby Boomers, Gen-Xers, and Millennials alike are spending more than 90% of their job search time online and 77%-87% of that online time is spent applying to jobs posted to job boards. We're spending about 85% of our time where only about 15% are located. Even if the numbers are moderately accurate, it's safe to conclude that changes in our job search habits need to occur.[17]

Topic	Type	Boomers	Gen-X	Millennials
Percent of Time Spent Searching and where	Online Offline	96% 4%	95% 5%	92% 5%
Primary Search Tool	Job Boards	87%	82%	77%

Despite arguments far and wide that this isn't the case, talk of the Hidden Job Market (myth or reality) persists. Detractors

[17] Dan Schwabble, The Multigenerational Job Search Study 2012, *Millennial Branding*, Sept. 24, 2012.

such as Gerry Crispen, an operator of CareerXroads and an employment consultant, claim, "Maybe a few thousand out of 20 million jobs are unpublished, and they are primarily at or near the C-level." (Note: I agree wholeheartedly with Mr. Crispen's assertion that lower level jobs are posted at a rate considerably higher than those of executive positions).[18]

On the other side of the coin, those who dismiss the Hidden Job Market as a myth fail to consider a few facts such as the expense of posting a job on most job boards (as much as $4,000-$18,000 per employee), or the cost of lost employee productivity reading through hundreds of applicants' resumes. Consider companies in America average only 16.3 employees so most companies don't have to abide by EEOC regulations.[19]

Then, there is networking and direct referrals. Some companies even have goals approaching 40% in their Employee Referral Programs (ERPs). Enterprise Rent-A-Car posts internal leaderboards showing which regions are referring the most candidates.

If that's not enough, there's the example of the TAM at the Southern Company, a Fortune 150 power generation company, who posted a requisition for an administrative assistant (HR jargon for they had a job for a secretary) and received in excess of 1,200 applications.[20]

---

[18] Katharine Hansen, PhD., Is the Hidden Job Market a Myth? The quintessential Careers Investigation of the Unpublicized Job Market, *LiveCareer*.

[19] United States Census Bureau, Section 15 Business Enterprise.
[20] Paul Petrone, 4 Steal-Worthy Secrets of Top Employee Referral Programs, LinkedIn, September 13, 2016.

Finally, when one considers just how quick and easy it is to find as many good candidates as you want using Boolean searches, it seems to me the Hidden Job Market should not be discounted.

Boolean Searches

Do you recall as a high school freshman math student saying, "I'll never use this stuff ever again in my entire life."? Yeah, me too. Boy, were we ever wrong! Mathematics is being used behind the scenes to find you as a candidate. More likely, it's keeping you from getting found. Let me explain.

Remember algebra's order of operations (that braces, brackets, and parenthesis thing)? It was invented by an English mathematician named George Boole. He lived only into his 49th year, and I bet his students hated him as much as we did. I can't confirm it, but it's my belief that he died at such a young age because he also accidently invented "texting" because his students took their math textbooks and *texted* him ... to death. (Don't worry, I get groans every time I tell that story.)

Tech geeks devised an adaptation of George Boole's order of operations to search for words. Every time you "Google" a product, company, service, or person, you are using this adaptation; you are conducting a Boolean search. This same theory is used in practice by Recruiters to find candidates and they can find as many qualified people for a job just as quickly as you uncover whatever you are looking for.

Come on Al!

A few years ago, I conducted a Boolean search live while speaking at a job networking event. I told those in attendance, "Just like a Recruiter, I can find as many people as I want to fill any job and I can do it in a matter of minutes." You may be as skeptical as they were.

For the exercise, I told the group a new pharmaceutical company with a blockbuster new drug was moving its headquarters to Zip Code 30317 (the northern Atlanta suburb of Sandy Springs where I was speaking). It needed a Vice President of Sales with new product launch experience who lived within a 25-mile radius. I told the participants I would use LinkedIn to fill the position. (Sound reasonable?)

So, just like a Recruiter would, I started my search by typing the first part of the title: "Vice President." Can you believe there were more than 56,000 people with the title of Vice President within that 25-mile radius? Then I added sales: "vice president of sales." The number dropped to 22,000 +/- people. (Note the terms are in quotes. When in quotes, the terms must show up in that order. It's called a long-tailed string of keywords. If not in quotes, the search's results might include the President of the United States, vice cops, and every sales person on earth.)

Next, I went to the keyword section, and just like a Recruiter would, I began entering terms to parse-down my results. I added AND "new product launch" where the results were chopped down to 1,200. When I added AND pharmaceutical the number dropped to 91. Finally, I added NOT insurance (this term eliminated people with an insurance background). The final number was nine. All the people I uncovered were perfect for the fictitious job I created; eight of the nine were brilliant, and one of them was me. Recruiters do the same thing every day.

Why do they do that?

Time. TAMs are doing the work that two to three people used to do. By using Boolean searches, TAMs can find as many qualified candidates as they need to fill virtually any position without ever posting a job, reading through hundreds of resumes (even a thousand), or handling countless calls. Unfortunately, this also means that many exceptionally qualified people are overlooked because don't have the right keywords in the right quantity to get found. Sound familiar?

Keep in mind how this is done: TAMs start with the job title they are seeking to fill, then add a handful of keywords to parse the results down to a manageable number of candidates. Fall inside that number and you are likely to get a call. You will not get a call if you don't have the searched title and/or those specific keywords <u>in quantity</u>.

Prove it!

Better than me, how about we let a real-life explain how Boolean searches work? June Burchfield is a Recruiter and friend who is also a volunteer at Roswell UMC Job Networking. She jumped at the opportunity to share how Boolean searches work for Recruiters and, therefore, how they can be adapted to your benefit. Here's June with "**Boolean Search Logic**":

Boolean search logic helps Recruiters search quickly for qualified candidates. Recruiters use Boolean search strings to look for certain keywords and/or phrases. They also use it to *exclude* certain keywords. Using Boolean search strings can take a pool of candidates from 1,000 to under 50 in the flash of an eye.

There are six main functions that Recruiters use to create Boolean search strings.

1. AND Function - Finds two or more words in a database.
   a. Example: Sales AND B2B AND Director
   b. All three words must be on a candidate's resume to populate in the Recruiter's search.
2. Quotation Marks Function - Finds an exact phrase. Prevents the search from pulling a candidate who has those words but not together.
   a. Example: "XYZ Company"

b. Only people with the exact phrase of XYZ Company will pull up. I also use "Recent college graduate" when looking to place entry-level positions.

3. OR Function - Finds either keyword.
   a. Example: Sales OR Marketing
   b. If the word Sales or Marketing is on a candidate's resume, it will populate in the search. Or, is also useful for commonly misspelled keywords such as "Power Point" OR PowerPoint.
4. NOT Function - Excludes a keyword.
   a. Example: Technician NOT Diesel
   b. If a candidate has Technician on his/her resume and the word diesel, s/he won't populate in the search.
5. * Function - Used to find all variations of a keyword.
   a. Example: Recruit*
   b. This will find the keywords recruit, recruits, recruited, Recruiter, recruiting, etc.
6. Parentheses Function - Used to create more complex search strings.
   a. Example: Sales AND (B2B OR "Business to Business") Not Director
   b. This search will find candidates who have Sales and either B2B or Business to Business but not Director on their resume.

It's important to have keywords on your resume to ensure Recruiters find you. Also, be mindful to change your job title on your resume to reflect what is common in your industry. Recruiters won't look for "Multi-Unit Manager," but they will look for "Regional Manager."

Boolean searches can also help you as a job seeker. Use them on Google, LinkedIn, Monster, and CareerBuilder to narrow your job search. A quick search on Monster for Sales positions in Atlanta, Georgia, pulls 1,000+ positions. Adding Sales AND

B2B lowers that number to 726. Updating to Sales AND B2B AND Director lowers that number to 5.

Search your top keywords to see if they are relevant or just taking up valuable space on your resume. A quick search on Monster for Sales AND Manager AND recruit shows 2 positions. When we change it to Sales AND Manager NOT recruit, we get 42 positions. Test your search strings slowly as *, quotations, and parentheses don't always work. Start with one or two keywords first. Then make your search more complex to narrow from 1,000 positions to a more reasonable number.

Keep in mind, most Recruiters are paid on commission, so they need to find, contact, and place the best candidates as quickly as possible (before other Recruiters find them). Now you see why smart Recruiters use Boolean search strings; they uncover qualified candidates while shortening search times dramatically.

In this chapter, you will learn to turn what had worked only for Recruiters to your benefit for both your resume and your online profiles, but first we need to discuss "the Black Hole."

Brain Without a Heart

In his seminal novel, *1984,* George Orwell wrote about the country of *Oceania,* where the people were constantly watched, even in their own home, through the use of "telescreens." The leader, known only as Big Brother, was always watching. Orwell's timing was only off by a few years. Welcome to the age of Artificial Intelligence; Oceania is here.

What is Artificial Intelligence?

Artificial Intelligence (AI) is a branch of computer science where computers are "taught" to simulate (imitate) intelligent human behavior. It's here today and is being increasingly used in all sorts of human endeavors, including, but not limited to, hiring.

Jennifer Alsever, in her eye-opening *Fortune Magazine* article, "Where Does the Algorithm See You in 10 Years?" states that algorithms are used to speed-up the vetting process and determine "book knowledge" and even more intangible qualities. AI uses "natural-language processing and machine learning to construct a psychological profile that predicts whether a person will fit the company culture."[21]

Currently, speed seems to draw first blood, "We can look at 4,000 candidates and within a few days whittle it down to the top 2% to 3%, forty-eight hours later, someone is hired." But, quick turnaround is only one of the desirable factors for companies. Predictions can be made on all sort of human qualities by observing candidates' word choice, micro-gestures, psycho-emotional traits, and the tone of their social media posts.

On the positive side, some biases can be programmed out of the initial hiring process. Sight-unseen, better candidates can be brought to the attention of Talent Acquisition and Hiring Managers without the bias of gender, race, and other personal identifiers clouding the initial decision-making process.

Other positives include common myths are being disproved with science, such as:

1. **Degrees are Required:** GPA's and test scores are worthless according to Google's own research. Companies are increasingly hiring people without a college degree. Up to 14% of some teams never went to college.
2. **IQ is King:** University of Pennsylvania found grit, passion, and persistence were better predictors of a person's

[21] Jennifer Anserver, How AI is Changing Your Job Hunt, *Fortune*, May 29, 2017.

enduring success and people from tough neighborhoods fared better than looks, health, IQ, and social intelligence.

3. **Experience is Everything:** The American Assn. of Inside Sales Professionals concluded that graduates with mid-level extracurriculars outperformed team leaders because companies need team players more than stars.
4. **A Star is a Star is a Star:** Match and fit are better predictors of success than doing well elsewhere. (This is something they would have to prove to me.)
5. **Boozers are Bad:** The AI company Fama found that pictures of drinking didn't imply bad job performance. On the other hand, comments of a bigoted nature or about drugs were linked to below-average performance.

I'm not completely ready to give in to Big Brother yet, but one is foolish indeed if s/he doesn't seek to get an in-depth understanding of how companies find candidates and position oneself to get found. If they don't find you, they'll find someone else.

Speaking of getting found, are you submitting your resume and applying to job postings you're perfect for but getting nowhere? If so, let me introduce you to the Black Hole.

Applicant Tracking Systems

Applicant Tracking System (ATS) software packages scan submissions (job applications and/or resumes) for the keywords programmed into the software to see if what is written matches what companies are seeking.

I facilitate a Resume Writing Workshop. In it, I use a slide showing the "Top 10" ATSs from a few years ago. In preparation for this book, I did a search: "Top 100 Applicant Tracking System software packages." I clicked on the first result that didn't say ad. I went to softwareadvice.com, where it compared 258 software packages![22]

For a few years I cited the statistic in my Resume Workshop, "60% of American companies use some sort of ATS." That number is out of date. According to Preptel, 60-70% of companies used ATSs in 2012 with the number approaching 90% as of 2015.[23] If that's not enough, in a 2014 *Recruiting Daily* article, Lachezar Stamatov claimed, "Seventy-five percent (75%) of big companies use ATSs. With the price of these packages dropping, their prevalence can only be on the rise.[24]

Don't believe me alone. Here's Recruiter June Burchfield's take of the uses of ATSs:

> **A**n Applicant Tracking System is simply software that a company uses to manage its recruitment process. Applicant Tracking Systems (ATS) are used by over 75% of companies. They are a necessity for companies to stay organized with candidates. I recently posted a sales position and got over 100 submissions the first day. A good ATS helped me weed through the plethora of resumes so that I could find qualified candidates.
>
> How a Recruiter uses an ATS can vary. The three main uses are:
>
> 1. Post new job openings for candidates to apply to along with pre-screening questions.
> 2. Search for candidates already in the ATS when new positions become available.
> 3. Search through candidates who applied for the job.

---

[22] Top Applicant Tracking Systems, Software Advice.

[23] Rezi Advice, 7 Myths About Applicant Tracking Systems, Jul. 1, 2015.

[24] Noel Cocca, Why Every Recruiter Should Use an Applicant Tracking System, *Recruiting Daily*, August 22, 2014.

Remember my sales example? My ATS flagged 20 out of 100 candidates with sales experience and only 10 out of 100 with Business-to-Business (B2B) sales experience; and 90% of my candidates were unqualified.

There are simple ways to get your resume through an ATS and get that dream job.

- **Be qualified for the position.** There's always a story of a friend of a friend of your cousin's uncle who was hired for a job they weren't qualified for, but that's an urban myth. The person didn't get hired because s/he merely applied; s/he was hired because of knowing somebody at that company.
- **Answer the prescreening questions.** Be honest in your replies. If you don't have the experience, you'll be found out quickly through a phone screen.
- **Upload your resume in an ATS-friendly format.** Word or PDF is best. You can also use a downloaded Google Doc or text document. Don't take a picture of your resume or use a scanned image of your resume. An ATS won't recognize the format. You will lose out on being keyword matched. If a Recruiter finds your resume on Monster, CareerBuilder, et al., and it's a picture of your resume, the Recruiter can't upload it to his/her ATS. If the resume can't be uploaded, the Recruiter is not likely to call you.
- **Make sure relevant experience is on your resume,** even if it's over. Good Recruiters and Hiring Managers no longer adhere to the "one-page resume" rule. However, if you are 18, your resume shouldn't be five pages.

  A good Recruiter and Hiring Manager should be able to find your resume based on the above. Still, with an ATS, you are competing against at least 100 other candidates to get noticed. Getting through an ATS should be one of your job search tools, but it works best in conjunction with networking. There are a few other tidbits you need to keep in mind.

"The Rule of Three"

Not a month after publication of the initial HIRED! book, a Recruiter friend, Jay Boylan, asked me if I knew about the "Rule of Three." I asked, "What the hell is the 'Rule of Three'?"

Believe it or not, some ATSs are so complex they can be programmed to exclude submissions (resumes) that don't have the company's desired keywords three times. But, unlike virtually every resume writer, Recruiter, and job coach, we DO NOT want you to re-write your resume every time you want to apply for a job.

Sacrilege! Everyone says you MUST re-write your resume for every job you apply to!!!

Keep your pants on. Let's think about this for a minute. How long does it take to re-write your resume? How many jobs do you apply to on a weekly basis during transition? If you do what they're telling you to do, you could become a "professional resume changer" (trust me, the salary stinks and the benefits suck hot dog water), you will screw-up your resume (you'll take good stuff out and forget to put it back in) and you'll never be able to keep up with what resume you sent to which company.

Instead, I want you to be smarter than the average job seeker by going through the keyword discovery process, Words-to-Work, outlined in this chapter AND adding a job-specific cover letter as a third page of your resume document. See, the combination of uncovering then loading your job title's keywords into your resume (and online profiles) will get you most of the way, but by adding a one-page cover letter written specifically for the job you're applying to will dramatically increase your chances of getting through the Black Hole. We'll walk you through how to make it work for you, step-by-step, in the Cover Letter subchapter.

S.E.O. for YOU (Search Engine Optimization)

When you "Google" something, how many pages of search results do you look at? One page? Two pages? Maybe, from time to time, three?

When I Googled the line from *Romeo & Juliet* quoted earlier in this book, within a millisecond I received 111 million results. I looked at the first one. End of story. Sound familiar?

In her Searchenginewatch.com article, Jessica Lee reported that whatever placed Google page 1, position 1 in search results got 33% of all views, with position two getting 18%. Traffic declined precipitously from that point. (See charts from the search-targeted advertising company, Chitika, cited in Ms. Lee's article.) Indeed, 91.5% of all Google traffic in the USA and Canada goes to whatever is found on the first page of results and 4.8% going to what's on page 2. For obvious reasons, companies work tirelessly (and pay dearly) to get to page 1.[25]

---

[25] Jessica Lee, No. 1 Position in Google Gets 33% of Search Traffic, *Search Engine Watch*, Jan. 20, 2013.

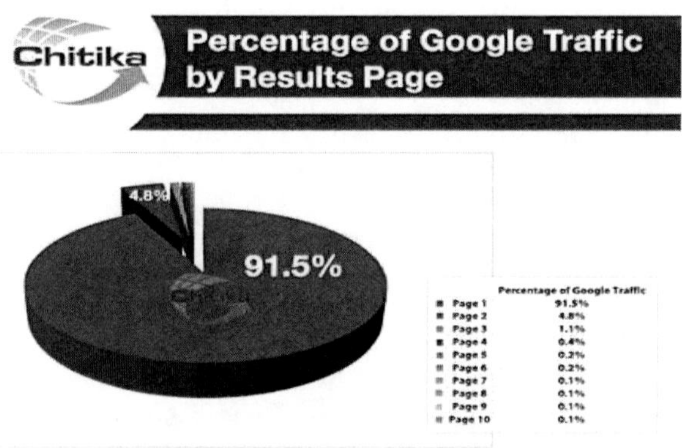

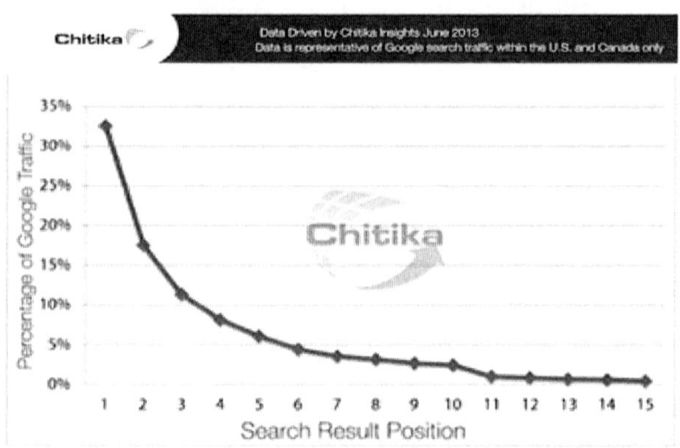

How do they get to Page 1?

One of the key methods to get to page 1 is through SEO: keywords. Although much more complicated, Google and the other search engines' algorithms pick up on keywords in your search terms and match them with results that contain those keywords. The "more optimized," the better the chance of being among the ones you click on.

What does that have to do with Job Search?

Everything! Because what works for Google works for job search.

Ever been fishing? Think about the similarities between fishing and job search. If you want to catch a fish or you want to get a job, you need something to attract your target audience. In fishing, we call it bait. In job search, we call it keywords.

We have established the following:

1. The vast majority of companies use some sort of ATS searching for keywords,
2. Some ATSs can be programmed so your submissions must satisfy the Rule of Three, where their selected keywords must appear three times in your submission, and
3. Recruiters can find as many qualified people as they want in moments by searching the job boards or online profiles (especially LinkedIn) through the use of Boolean searches comprised of keywords.

So, keywords are important

If you want to get found for the 82-85% of the jobs that are hidden, or you want to get through the Black Hole of online applications to reach the 15-18% of posted jobs, you MUST uncover the keywords for your job title of choice, then load your resume and online profiles with those keywords. You need the right words in the right quantity if you want to get work.

How do I do that?

"Words-to-Work" Page 1 Positioning

Let's start with a reminder of how Recruiters find candidates: They start with the job title they seek to fill then add keywords to parse the results to a manageable number. We will reverse the process that currently works only for Recruiters and make the same process work for you.

Because 93% of Recruiters use LinkedIn as their primary search tool, let's use LinkedIn.[26] Start with your desired job title. What title do you want next? As an example, suppose you want a job as Supply Chain Director. (Note: this process is a royal PITA, but it's effective for almost any title).

Follow these steps:

1. Type your desired job title into the search bar on your LinkedIn Homepage. (in the example, I type supply chain director)
2. In LinkedIn's current iteration, you should have three choices among which to choose: Jobs with the title supply chain director, People with the title supply chain director, or Groups about supply chain directors. Choose Jobs for the title supply chain director. At this moment in time, LinkedIn shows 684 jobs posted nationwide searching for a Supply Chain Director. Time to parse this down a bit to get closer to what you want.
3. On the right-hand side of the page, you can narrow your search. The first option is location and although it's tempting to look only in your area, resist. You should be looking for WORDS, not work right now. The next option is for specific companies; do not look here either. If you are a Premium member, your next option is salary range. This is a good choice, but we will assume you haven't paid for premium. Go all the way down to Industry and choose yours. I will choose Consumer Goods. Click your choice.
4. When I did, 51 positions appeared. Now the PITA part begins. Begin reading the job description of the first job. If it is a "perfect" fit for you, set it aside for a bit. If it's not perfect, go on to the next one (you have 50 more from which to choose)
5. When you find 3-5 perfect jobs (despite the location and/or company), you can stop

---

[26] JobVite, Jobvite Social Recruiting Survey Finds Over 90% of Employers Will Use Social Recruiting in 2012, Jul. 9, 2012.

6. Open a Word document (or Apple's equivalent)
7. Copy each of the job descriptions into your document (I suggest you skip a page between job descriptions).
8. Delete the EEOC disclaimers
9. Delete the material about the specific company
10. Delete words such as Requirements, preferred, skills, education, experience, and other equally superfluous terms.
11. Go to a Word Cloud generator (Wordle.net is the largest, but Wordle is in java script and some computers have trouble with that program). ABCYA.com/word_clouds.htm is the word cloud generator I prefer. Yes, it's a word cloud generator for kids, but with me being as childish as I am, it's a perfect fit.
12. Copy all the material in your Word document and enter it into the word cloud generator
13. Click to make a word cloud.
14. One of the reasons I prefer ABCYA is because it offers options to make your word cloud into black type on a white background (lower cost to print), change the orientation to horizontal (easier to read), and adjust the amount of words considered (allowing you to work with as many or as few words as desired).
15. Read through the word cloud for the most important words describing what you do. Pay little attention to the font size. Font size is relative to the number of times the word appears, not necessarily its relative importance. Choose the most important 10.
16. Add to your keyword list anything you know to be important, but somehow went missing AND add any acronyms as they are almost always important. Your list should be about 15-20 words.
17. Use these words to populate both your resume and online profiles.

(**Note**: I hate word clouds for many reasons. I pay for a different tool that produces a spreadsheet as opposed to a word cloud; but, word cloud generators are the best free services available.)

This is where most people stop. Not us. Now you need to compare your profile to that of your "competition."

This really is a PITA. Am I done now?

Sorry, no. Because of the algorithmic weight given job titles, you need to use your desired job title as many times as possible throughout your profile. You should also create a "current" job.

What if I don't have a job?

Hang with me a minute. You need to create a "current" job on LinkedIn that states you are seeking that position. By doing this, you will not be excluded when Recruiters conduct a search. Many will parse out anyone who doesn't currently have the title they are trying to fill.

What if I have a job, but I'm looking?

You certainly don't want to get caught seeking greener pastures. What I suggest is to add a line something like this, "Gained a reputation for always seeking new opportunities to add bottom line profitability for my company (or something like that).

Can I really do this?

In most cases, yes. As I said earlier, the process is a pain, but it can be done and is effective for almost every title and industry.

My personalized "Words-to-Work" clients MUST be somewhere on the first half of page one when I conduct a Boolean search before I "release" them. Of course, there's more to the process, but what I have stated here is the nuts and bolts.

What if I can't do it?

If you have difficulty, contact me, "I can be rented." My website is: theHIREDguy.com. Send a Linkedin connection request while you're at it. We will work together until you are on page 1 any time a Recruiter does a search for your desired job title.

"Life is like riding a bicycle.
To keep your balance,
you must keep moving"
-Albert Einstein

Chapter 6: LinkedIn & Other Social Media

"The trouble with a target-rich environment is that it's useless if you don't know which target you have to aim at."
-Terry Pratchett

Social Media Overview

There are a gazillion social media platforms, many of which post jobs. You can make yourself crazy trying to position yourself on all of them, so it's my recommendation to choose a couple of places to stake your claim and then focus your effort there. Love or hate social media, at least a couple platforms must be part of your Marketing Campaign.

Recruiters regularly use social media to find candidates (they also use social media to exclude people, so keep this in mind). I've seen numbers as high as 97% of Recruiters use some sort of social media in their searches. (This number likely includes both seeking candidates for positions and researching personal and professional negatives.) A couple of years ago, Jobvite conducted a survey of Recruiters and found 93% of Recruiters used LinkedIn as their *primary* search tool (that means BEFORE a resume!). Jobvite's National Recruiter Survey 2015 results are similar, with LinkedIn still leading the pack. Interestingly, Recruiters aren't afraid of using smaller platforms, including Snapchat, Vimeo, Periscope, or Tumblr. Here are results of *how Recruiters find qualified candidates*:

92%	Social Media (some form)
87%	LinkedIn
55%	Facebook
47%	Twitter

Traditionalists shouldn't be alarmed because 78% of those surveyed stated their best candidates are still found by referral. Indeed, many companies have referral programs and, as previously mentioned, some pay referral bonuses.[27]

Before you go hog-wild posting to social media sites, keep in mind George Orwell only missed it by a few years: Big Brother is most certainly watching you as is evidenced in a 2014 CareerBuilder article where Rosemary Haefner states, "Forty-three percent of employers use social networking sites to research job candidates. The employers who are already searching sites aren't impressed with what they're finding, which has potentially serious implications for job seekers. Fifty-one percent of employers who research job candidates on social media say they've found content that led them to **not** hire the candidate, up from 43 percent last year and 34 percent in 2012."[28]

I've been the moderator (or "Community Leader") for a few LinkedIn groups, including an alumni group. There was one joker who would post racist and sexist comments, so I sent him a note saying if he ever wanted to get a job, he needed to cut his nonsense out. I got the response I anticipated *"First Amendment! First Amendment!"* (I am happy to say, to the best of my knowledge, he still doesn't have a job! I'm not fond of bigots, can you tell?)

More Orwellian statistics:

- 48% of employers will use Google or other search engines to research candidates
- 44% will research the candidate on Facebook
- 27% will monitor the candidate's activity on Twitter
- 23% review the candidate's posts or comments

---

[27] Kimberlee Morrison, Survey: 92% of Recruiters Use Social Media to Find High-Quality Candidates, *ADWeek*, Sep. 22, 2015.

[28] Rosemary Haefner, Think before you post: Your online presence can cost you a job, CareerBuilder, June 26, 2014.

- Much of this research happens **PRIOR** to a phone screen or interview

My recommendation is to schedule regular, monthly check-ups. See if there is anything untoward about you on the main social media platforms. Begin by entering your name in quotation marks. Check all options: news, videos, images, personal. If you uncover something negative, especially on the first three pages, see if it can be removed. If you can't, try drowning the bad stuff off the first few pages by creating new content. (Note: If you're on Google, sign out before conducting your audit. The same pertains to the other search engines.)

Aliza Licht, in *Forbes*, suggested 5 ways to clean-up your social media footprint:[29]

1. Google Yourself (where did I hear that before?)
2. Spring Clean - Delete posts that don't fit your rep.
3. Email Etiquette - Are you negative, or do you inspire?
4. Manage your Bio - Write a bio of who you are and what you do
5. Amplify your Name - Publish content (familiar?)

None of this is meant to persuade you from using social media platforms as part of your job search Marketing Campaign. On the contrary, it would be foolish NOT to be where Recruiters are looking for candidates. In fact, not having a social media footprint can harm your chances! What we are saying is to be smart and stay professional:

- No religion
- No politics
- No off-color jokes
- No drinking or drugs
- No questionable photographs

[29] Aliza Licht, Five Ways to Improve Your reputation in 2017, *Women Forbes*, Jan. 4, 2017.

All that aside, it's time to create professional online profiles to showcase what you bring to the table for prospective employers.

LinkedIn Overview

At this moment in time, LinkedIn is a must for serious job seekers, as is evidenced by the fact that approximately 90% of Recruiters use LinkedIn as their primary search tool. Anyone without a LinkedIn profile is pretty much dead in the water. That being said, most people's LinkedIn profiles are like a certain part of one's anatomy: we all have one and they stink.

While I don't profess to be a LinkedIn expert (I possess a distrust for self-proclaimed experts; and with LinkedIn's proclivity for making radical changes, I am exceptionally suspect of anyone claiming to be a LinkedIn guru).

I don't care one bit about the microbiology of LinkedIn or other social media platforms and I will not bore you with all that garbage. What I'm going to focus on is what you NEED to know about LinkedIn to be successful.

The French Maid (Some things can't be unseen)

We'll start by assuming you have some sort of LinkedIn profile. If not, sign up and follow along (you're not as far behind as you might think). In either case, I recommend you do most of your profile creation offline in a Word document or its Apple equivalent. The reason is that you should be able to minimize and catch errors easier. But, before you create your first line of text, there are a few pieces of housekeeping that need to be attended to, section by section (Note: I will be focusing only on the parts I believe are important for job search. Feel free to explore further, if desired).

In my "Words-to-Work" workshops, I tell the participants that we have some housekeeping to do prior to getting into the W2W process. I have a clip art slide of a French maid at this point of the presentation. My story about the French Maid is that I work out of my home office as much as possible and my wife asks me to clean the place. (Sounds fair enough, right?). I get a call one morning, "Hey, Al, what are you doing?" I respond, "I just slipped into my French Maid outfit."

Arrrrrgh!!! Al, I'm scratching my eyes out!

Now that I've blinded you, I'll lead you step-by-step through some important preliminary housekeeping you should complete prior to re-writing your profile. Open your LinkedIn profile and we'll get started:

1. Go to your Home Page, **click on the small picture** toward the top right-hand side
2. Click on **Privacy & Settings** in the dropdown box (You will enter the Basics section)
3. Click **Email addresses**. I recommend 2 email addresses. Click **Close** when done.
4. Click **Phone numbers**. Add phone numbers of your choice. Click **Close** when done.

Other, Optional Steps:

5. Click **Saving job application answers**. This may save time when applying to jobs posted on LinkedIn. Click **Close** when done.
6. (recommended) Click **Get an archive of your data**. Click **Fast file and other data**. The best reason to acquire this information is to have a record of your contacts. Click **Close** when done.
7. Click **Twitter settings**. If you have a Twitter account (you should), you may want that address known to readers of your profile. **Click back arrow**.

One section down. Now on to the **Privacy** section.

1. Click **Privacy** (Adjacent to Basic on top row)
2. Click **Who can see your connections**. I recommend you keep your connections totally private; if you agree, click **Only you**. Click **Close** when done.
3. Click **Viewers of this profile also viewed**. Slide button to **No** from Yes (Yes is the default setting). This is one of the most important settings for you to change permanently. As you add connections and improve your profile, you will increasingly attract Recruiters to your profile. The ten people listed can be competitors to you in your job search. Recruiters LOVE seeing those people. Unfortunately for you, Recruiters can venture away from your profile and never come back. Click **Close** when done.
4. Click **Sharing profile edits**. Slide from Yes to **NO** (TEMPORARILY!!!). Every time you make a change to your profile you must click Save. If you share all the changes necessary to make your profile a real winner, you may be seen as a spammer. It's important to staple a note to your forehead to change this back to Yes when you are satisfied with your changes because from that point forward you want to make as much noise and attract as much attention as possible. (**Write a note NOW to turn back to Yes as a reminder.)** Click **Close** when done.
5. Click **Profile viewing options**. There are three options. I recommend you maintain full visibility. If you want to do some "snooping" later, you can change to either of the anonymous modes then change back at any time. Click **Close** when done.
6. Click **Let recruiters know you're open to new opportunities**. Move to **Yes**. Certainly, if you are not employed, you want this option on; but, if you have a job, I recommend you have this in the **No** mode because LinkedIn can't guarantee your current employer won't discover your option ... and many look! Click **Close** when done.

There's much more you can explore, but I want to stick to the basics for getting started.

LinkedIn (What you NEED to know)

Photograph

Sometimes the simplest things are minimized, overlooked, or never completed. Let's start with one of those simple things: a photograph.

Why do I need a photograph?

A photograph isn't required by LinkedIn; but, not having one can hurt your chances of getting your profile viewed. Many people, me included, do not accept connection requests from people without a photograph and I tend not to allow such people into the groups I moderate. Big deal? Well, according to LinkedIn's research, "Posting a profile photo is optional, but it helps your connections and others recognize you. In fact, members with profile photos receive 14 times more profile views than those without." Convinced? (You can find this quote in LinkedIn's Help section)

Not a problem. I got some photos in my phone.

LinkedIn is "the world's largest **professional** networking site," remember? So, your LinkedIn photograph should be a part of your professional branding statement. If you work in a suit and tie, wear one in your profile photo. If you work in a more casual atmosphere, let your picture reflect that image. A professional headshot is worth the investment of a couple hundred bucks. Don't be a cheapskate! You DO NOT want:

- **The Facebook Look** - Where you crop out a friend with their arm around you.
- **The Fido Foto** - You may love your pet, but this isn't the place for "Phydeaux" (Cajun for Fido)
- **The Family Affair** - This isn't the place for a family photograph.

- **Fame or Fakery** - Using a famous cartoon character might be fine for YouTube, but not for LinkedIn; neither is a fake photo. (The "F-Grade" alliteration intended.)

A few parting notes about the LinkedIn headshot you choose:

1. Your face should take up about 60% of the photo,
2. It should be a good representation of what you look like today,
3. You should either lean in or look slightly to one side or the other. Shadows make a 2-dimensional image appear more 3-dimensional
4. Smile and try to engage your audience. Looks matter.
5. Looking slightly to the right guides readers to the body of your profile.

Background Image

LinkedIn allows you to upload an image. It can (and should) speak to your Brand. I use a piece of my book since my Brand is that I'm known as the HIRED! Guy.

When you go to your profile, there is a prompt to the right of your picture and the little pencil. Because I have a background image, my prompt reads: Update background photo (If you do not have a background image, it likely reads Upload background photo). When you click on the icon, three options appear.

1. Camera - Click here to upload an image (You can use most anything as your background, but LinkedIn suggests images with a resolution of 1536 X 768 (whatever that means).
2. Up/Down Arrow - Allows you to reposition the image to get as much of what you want seen as possible
3. Trash can - click here if you want to delete the image.

Congratulations, you have just completed the initial impression visitors of your profile will take away when they find you.

Intro Section

The "Intro" section is a combination of the previous Heading and Summary sections. To access your Intro section, click on the small picture of yourself ("Me") on the upper right-hand side of your Home Page then click **View Profile**. To edit your Intro, click on the little pencil in that first section. When you do, you will be directed to a new page where you will want to fill out the following:

1. **Name** - Use the name you go by professionally. You want to be found! I'm known as Al Smith even though the name I must use on my books is Alfred M. Smith (if you look up either Al Smith or Alfred Smith, you'll undoubtedly get page after page of results of the 1928 Democratic candidate for president, Alfred E. Smith. Gee, thanks, Dad!)
2. **Headline** - Enter the title you want next! (In almost every case.) If you are currently employed, you will probably want to have your current title.

   What if I don't have a job?

   You'll want to "create" a current job. The reason for this has to do with a couple things. First, the algorithm is heavily weighted toward both titles and current title. Second, many Recruiters add the term *AND current* to their search criteria to ensure the candidates they uncover can fill the Recruiter's requisition. If you don't have that title currently, you will be excluded from their search results. In this section, you can also include other things about yourself. (Note: I'll show how in a moment)
3. **Current Position** - Enter your current position (again). You want to take full advantage of the algorithm. This section will include the company you're working for currently. If you're not currently employed, you can make your employer your initials or at Currently seeking new opportunities (as your employer).

4. **Education** - You can enter any number of schools, but only one appears. My suggestion is to enter the most prestigious institution. (Note: naming a school isn't required and I have worked with many very talented people without a degree!).
5. **Zip Code** - Enter your postal code. (Note: If you live in one city and plan to move to another, use a postal code from that new city.)
6. **City** - In most cases, I recommend using the large city closest to where you reside. If you live in Aurora, Colorado, use Greater Denver. Recruiters know where Denver is, maybe not Aurora. (**Note:** Once again, if you want to move to a city other than where you currently live, enter that new city here)
7. **Industry** - There are a variety of general industries to choose among from a dropdown menu. I find them rather limiting, but we must deal with it. Choose the one closest to your desired industry.
8. **Summary** - This is the first place where all that "Words-to-Work" effort will come into place. First, you want to tell a story ... your story ... but do so by using the keywords you uncovered from the job descriptions and those you know are important. This section and the subsequent experience sections need to be keyword rich. You want to "out SEO" your competition, but you must do this in normal prose, NOT in blocks of the same word(s) repeated ad nauseum. (There was someone who sold these blocks of the same word garbage as a "service" promising to get clients to page 1 position 1. She got the people there, but most Recruiters figured, "If you scam us now, you'll scam us later." I also recommend you include contact information in your summary as well as in the contact information section. Make it easier for Recruiters and you're likely to get more calls! (Note: Adding a list of skills, all keywords, is acceptable.)
9. **Media** - This is one of the opportunities for keeping a Recruiter's attention when s/he discovers your profile. You

can upload a file or a link to media. (In my case, one of each). As an example of a file, all my clients must have a Value Proposition deck showcasing (in brief) what they bring to the table for a company. I highly recommend you do the same! (Note: More on Value Proposition decks later in this chapter) Many people want to upload their resume. I recommend you do not. What I want for you is to get a call from a Recruiter asking for your resume. What is it called when a Recruiter speaks to you … oh yeah, it's called an interview!

10. **Share Profile Edits** - As previously mentioned, while you are heavily building your profile, you should turn this option to no. Every time you click to save, the changes would otherwise go out to your entire network and you don't want to be seen as a spammer.
11. **Save** - When satisfied, click Save.

<u>Your Articles & Activity</u>

The next section, as currently structured, is Your Articles & Activity. Every time you write an article published on LinkedIn and any time you have activity (See: **Post to Start a Conversation** located toward the top of your Homepage) that activity will populate this section. Every time you post a conversation or activity, all your followers (also listed in this section) will be sent a notice of that activity. Every time someone Likes or Comments on it, your entire network of followers will "see" that piece again. A way you can increase the number of times your material repeats is either to thank people who comment or like your material and/or ask those who like the bit what they liked about it. Yes, it's a little underhanded, but effective at getting your works seen.

<u>Experience</u>

Just as you did in the Summary of your Intro section, you will keyword-load this entire section. We'll continue to work from your Profile section by clicking on the blue plus sign to add your new **Current** job.

But Al, aren't you the guy who says never lie?

Yes, I am. And you will NOT be telling anything but the truth! Hang with me a bit; it will all become clear to you. Trust me!

1. **Title** - Enter the title you want next. Remember how Recruiters search: they start with the job title in their requisition. You can have more than one title, but if you take this tact, those titles should be very similar, so you don't confuse your audience.
2. **Company** - If you have a company name, enter it. If you don't, create one.
3. **Location** - State your city (e.g., Greater New York, NY)
4. **From & To** - (I'm combining these two sections) You are prompted to state the month of your start date. I would resist if LinkedIn is currently allowing you to NOT enter the month. On the **To** side, click Present.
5. **I currently Work Here** - Slide this to Yes
6. **Description** - Describe what you can do for your next company, what you want to do, what you bring to the table (a history of award-winning, languages, specific experience, etc.) You can include what you have been doing during your period of transition. One client said, *"For the past 12 months I have been caring for my terminally ill mother. I was the only member of my family capable to step away from my professional responsibilities. Those duties are now complete, and I'm prepared to return to what I do best, manage a team of engineers, namely as Vice President of Engineering for your company."* (There was more to this section, but any Recruiter reading this experience would have to conclude he's a good guy and he had a plausible reason for his period of unemployment. You, too, can make this and all your experience come to life! (Full of keywords!) BTW: At some point, in this section add that you are seeking (or looking for) a job with this title. (See, you didn't tell a fib at all!)

7. **Media** - Once again, you can upload a link to media such as a video you have created then uploaded to YouTube (for example) for a second bite at your Value Proposition deck, a PowerPoint, or Slideshare.
8. **Share Profile Change** - This should be turned to the No position
9. **Save** - Click Save

Continue filling out this section by clicking the little blue pencil to edit your experience throughout this section. Use your keywords in quantity and add your desired title in parenthesis whenever possible, without lying, especially if the job you did had a different title, but your duties were the same. (**Note:** If you had multiple titles during your tenure at a company, enter each title as a separate job. You will have thousands of extra characters to play with for your keyword loading).

One more thing to note: LinkedIn allows you to have more than one current job!

If you have had multiple titles at a single employer, you can create an "experience" for the entirety of your tenure, then the most recent title at the company, then the next most recent, and so on. Each entry will give you another set of characters to fill with keywords. Again, it's a bit underhanded, but they created the game, I just "read the rulebook" and want you to take advantage of what I learned.

Education

By clicking on the plus sign, you can add an educational institution, degree(s) earned, overall field of study, activities and societies, and grades.

The less professional experience you have, the more important your education is to Recruiters. For recent college graduates, I recommend listing several courses taken within your chosen professional field. Also include papers and projects you worked on/completed for your field.

By clicking on the pencil, you can make changes to that which is existing. Remember to click Save when complete.

I recommend against mentioning your high school. There isn't any reason to differentiate between traditional and executive degrees. I also recommend against including years (unless it's to your advantage to do so).

Volunteer Experience

Volunteering is more than a feel-good activity. Many executives who volunteer prefer to surround themselves with people who give to their community and others. Doing so during transition "fills the gaps" and speaks highly of you.

Add any volunteerism, especially if it adds to your experience level or shows you are keeping your skills honed.

Featured Skills & Endorsements

This section is hated by Recruiters and its importance has been minimized by LinkedIn (for good reason). Endorsements are, however, part of the algorithm used to move your placement towards position one. (It wouldn't surprise me if this section is removed in the near future.)

You can add endorsements by clicking Add a new skill then type the skill where prompted, then click save. We recommend you use many of your chosen keywords as your skills.

By clicking the pencil, you can change the order of your skills. At this point, only three endorsements are visible without clicking "see more," so choose wisely.

Recommendations

If endorsements mean nothing to Recruiters, recommendations are both of great value and fully searchable for them. You should also note that both the number of recommendations you have given and received are listed. Giving recommendations means you are engaged with your network.

Ask your connections to write a recommendation of your work or character so it can be displayed on your profile. Here's how:

1. Go to the member's profile
2. Click on the **More** icon (3 dots) in the top section of the profile on the right-hand side of the picture
3. Click on **Request a recommendation**
4. Fill out **Relationship** and **Position at the time** fields of the pop-up box then click **Next**
5. You can change the text in the message field or even write the recommendation you desire, then click **Send**

The recommendations section is only displayed once you give or receive a recommendation that isn't hidden. You can request a recommendation from as many as three members at once, but there's no limit on the total number of recommendations you can request, give, or receive.

Proactively recommending someone is done in a similar manner as requesting a recommendation, starting with clicking the More button (three dots) and following the instructions.

<u>Accomplishments</u>

This section contains many subjects for you to consider adding including:

- Publications (add keyword loaded descriptions)
- Courses (given and taken)
- Languages (proficiency can be added ... or not)
- Projects

<u>Interests</u>

What are you interested in? Which influencers and others do you want to follow? What groups do you want to be a member of? You may choose as few or as many as you want. But let's focus on Groups. I recommend you become an active member of at least 4 industry groups and join as many others as you want.

Are Groups really that important?

Recruiters have been known to become a member of a group when they have a requisition to fill. They troll groups for thought leaders (people beginning and contributing to conversations, formerly called posts). As a matter of fact, a few years ago LinkedIn research found that top contributors to groups had their profiles read at a rate 400% greater than other group members.

Not only can groups expand your network, the titles of your groups can enhance positioning. Each group's title can become part of Boolean searches because they are found like every other keyword. Simply stated, your SEO is improved by the groups you are a member of and participate in.

Anchor Text in links

This was a new one on me. I found an excellent LinkedIn article by Bill Faeth, who explained, "Every LinkedIn profile '**Contact Info**' has a section where you can list up to three links. The default options include 'Company Website' and 'Blog,' but these aren't SEO-friendly. You can boost clicks by selecting the 'Other' option from the drop-down menu. If you want to link to your blog, use a keyword-rich title that explains *what* your blog is about, such as, *'My Supply Chain and Procurement Blog'*." Access the Contact Info section by clicking **Profile** > **Contact Info**, and clicking the pencil icon next to **Websites**.[30]

---

[30] Bill Faeth, Sneaky LinkedIn SEO Hacks to Boost Your Profile Views, Inbound Marketing Blog, December 3, 2015.

Contact and Personal Info

Just before I got back to the writing of this chapter, I checked a client's profile. I wanted to send his contact information to a Recruiter friend for a position she was working and for which my client would be a perfect fit. I wanted the Recruiter to check out the guy's profile before sending emails around. When I clicked on the "contact and personal info" section, the only things I found were his LinkedIn address (I needed that) and the website information for his FORMER company. Let's not make the same mistake (Yes, I sent him a note to fix the omissions).

Click on the little pencil in this area and add as many of the following as you want:

- Website(s)
- Phone number (you want Recruiters to call, right?)
- Email (You want them to write, too!)
- Address (not me ... don't know why this is important)
- Twitter (yuck)
- Birth date (not for me)

Let's make it as easy as we can for Recruiters to learn more and contact you. Recruiters are doing the work of two or three people these days. If it's difficult for them to make contact; they are likely to just move on to the next candidate. Have your contact information in the Contact and personal information section, but also in your summary.

Saving some of the most important stuff for last

Home Page

Most of your work will begin from your Home Page. You need to become comfortable with it, so let's get to it. First, look for your picture on the left-hand side. Look for two sets of numbers (you may have only 1 set for now): Who's viewed your profile and Who's viewed your post. Both of these numbers matter.

<u>Who's viewed your profile</u>

Prior to LinkedIn's draconian changes in January 2017, this was easily the most important statistic provided for job seekers. Hopefully, by the time you read this book, LinkedIn will have returned a shorter-term time period than its current, virtually useless, 90-day number (I'll show more on what they have moved to later in the book). In case they have not yet ... **Help me, get the short-term number back:**

- Scroll down on your home page a little bit until you see a group of words in a box on the right-hand side of the page.
- Click Help Center
- Scroll down the page to the bottom
- Click Contact us
- On the new page, type: *Who's viewed your profile* in the blue outlined box.
- Click enter
- Click next
- Fill in your form
    - Issue type: click Searching
    - On what device: click LinkedIn (Website)
    - Your question: type "Please return the numbers on Who's viewed your profile to a daily number. The Current 90-day is useless for job seekers"

Now, back to business.

Click the number below **Who's viewed your profile.** You should see a couple columns. On the left should be the number of profile views over the previous 90-day period (divide by 13 to see what your weekly average is. For most people, your goal should be 20 views per week, but yours is likely to be way below that number). Below that, in either green or red, is a percentage up or down since last week (a virtually useless number). Below that should be how many people, at various companies, viewed your profile during the 90-day period. Clicking on them should reveal who they are. Connect with the ones you are not connected to by clicking connect (add a brief personal note).

The center column shows people who have viewed your profile. In the free version of LinkedIn, only 5 people are revealed. My suggestion for free basic members is to check and note this number multiple times per day. This will be especially important as you start getting more views because Recruiter views is the goal.

Speaking of Recruiters, seldom will their name appear. A few will be displayed as "Recruiter." Most Recruiters are in Anonymous mode, which shows in this section as In Private Mode. The way to see how many people in Private Mode viewed your profile is to scroll all the way down to the bottom of this section (it's a time-consuming PITA, but is a worthwhile exercise). The more people viewing your profile in Private Mode, the better!

Who's viewed your post

LinkedIn gives us ways to increase profile views. One of them is through posting activity you find interesting. This is a great way to get more views and be seen as a "Thought Leader." Let's assume you have a number below the heading **Who's viewed your post.** If so, you already know the benefits of activity.

When you click on the number, you will have options for seeing some limited analytics of who's seen what. You can choose among the **Articles** you have written and/or "reposted," **Posts** (activity you have shared with your network) or **All Activity** (both Articles and Posts).

As stated above, being active in groups can help you get found by Recruiters and TAMs. Accenture, the management consulting, tech services, and outsourcing company, mines groups for active group members, "Recruiting candidates is based in part on their activity and influence on social sites."[31]

One blogger going only by the name Jonathan claims to have increased his views by more than 500% after fully instituting a "Content Marketing campaign."[32] He would post industry-related content 3-5 times per day. LinkedIn claims that by investing four hours per week, one can increase viewership 1,300%!

I can't come up with all that content!

On your own, probably not, but there's a world of pertinent content at your fingertips and it can come directly into your inbox. All you need to do is set up Google Alerts (more on that in a subsequent chapter). So, get active and stay active in groups!

Connections You can't have too many connections, but having too few can kill your chances on many levels.

1. If you have fewer than 500+ connections, you're seen by Recruiters as not being able to keep up with the times. This goes for recent college graduates and other young candidates just as it makes mature job seekers appear as old farts.
2. Many groups won't admit people with fewer than 100 connections (I don't).
3. Many members (including me) will not connect with those who have less than 100 connections. Many of these profiles are fake.

---

[31] Melissa Korn, Are You a Social Media Star? Accenture is Looking For You, *Wall Street Journal*, Dec. 11, 2013.

[32] Jonathan (no last name given), How to Increase Your LinkedIn Profile Views by 500%, Profile Launch Pad.

4. With a small network of LinkedIn connections, you have a very difficult time finding people at target companies. These are people who you need to research prior to your interviews, conventions, or other meetings.
5. Most important of all, Recruiters can't find you!

If you're not close to the magical 500+ connection level, don't sweat it. Adding connections is one of the few things that's become easier since Microsoft bought LinkedIn in 2016. You no longer have to give a person's email address or answer questions about how you know the individual. You can click Connect (see below):

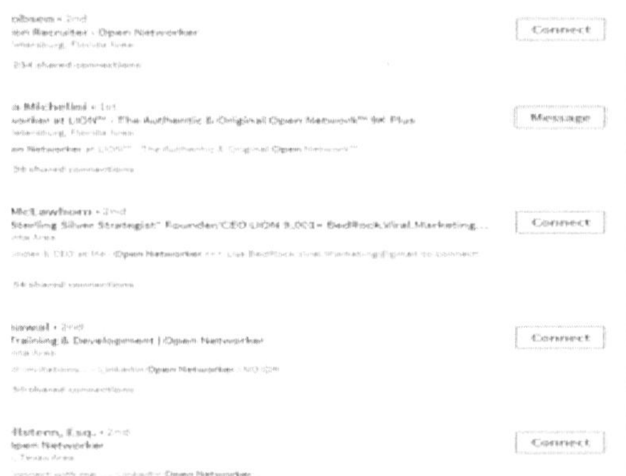

When you do a search, you can now click Connect with people to whom you are not currently connected. After you do, you will be asked if you want to send a message along with your request. I highly recommend doing this as many of us look askance at generic connection requests.
Note: I cropped people's picture and part of their name for privacy reasons.

A good way to quickly expand your connections in the short-term is to search for LION (LinkedIn Open Networkers) or conduct a search for people who have the term Open Networker. Just go to the white Search bar on your Home Page, type "open networker," click Enter, and start sending connection requests.

There are advantages for targeting LIONs and Open Networkers:

1. Most are Super Connectors with thousands of connections, who will make your network grow exponentially
2. Many will connect without viewing your profile, so you get more connections quicker.

There is a downside though, non-Premium members can quickly exceed their monthly "Maximum Search Limit." Although I'm not a fan of Premium memberships for people in job search, LinkedIn often offers deals of two months for the price of one (or one month free. I recommend taking advantage of these offers, then cancelling the service just before the promotion period is over).

Letting Recruiters Know

Under Privacy & Settings, scroll down to a section titled Job Seeking and under it there is a section titled Let Recruiters Know You're Open to Opportunities. This is an essential addition to your Marketing Campaign and should improve your profile view totals.

Here's how to turn the feature on:

1. **Click on your picture** on the top right side of your Home Page
2. Click Privacy & Settings in the dropdown box
3. Click **Settings** in the new screen
4. Scroll to **Job seeking**
5. Click on L**et Recruiters know you're open to opportunities**
6. Move button from Off to **On**
7. Add a detailed, keyword-filled note in section called **Note to Recruiters**

8. In section called, **What job titles are you considering**, add every iteration of the job title(s) you seek. Leave none out!
9. **What locations would you work in?** Name all cities and towns within your desired area
10. **What type jobs are you open to?** Of course, this is up to you, but I recommend adding contract to whatever else you want because this adds any contract-to-hire positions. Not clicking this will exclude you from those entirely.

Note: This feature may automatically turn off after 90 days, although I have seen notices from LinkedIn that it would be on for 180 days. In either case, this change may not be permanent.

Thanks to a successful client, Phil Nickerson, who pointed out the note above during a small group coaching call (he had already gotten his job offer too!). By mentioning this, he helped another member of the group increase Recruiter views to greater than 40% of her total.

Data Privacy & Advertising

MS Word now offers a Resume Assistant to help subscribers build a resume. Unfortunately, they might show your profile's wording to your competition. There's now a setting to combat this. In the **Privacy** section, Click: **Data privacy and advertising.** Then click:

Microsoft Word then slide the button from Yes to No. Moving the bar to No stops the sharing of the descriptions of experience you used in your profile with Microsoft Word users and will help prevent your information from being plagiarized.

Other Social Media: (Google, Twitter, Facebook, and others)

As the author Terry Pratchett said in the quote at the beginning of this chapter, you must choose your target(s) wisely. For that reason, you should choose which other social media sites you want to have a profile on. Facebook, Twitter and Google are certainly important entities. They have many posted jobs and draw much viewership. On the other hand, beware of spreading yourself too thin or relying too heavily on social media.

Don't get me wrong, social media (plural) is an exceptionally important set of tools. But, some people can get into social media so deeply it can become all-consuming and you have a job to do. Your job is to get a job! Get out there and mingle. Job search is still a "contact sport."

LinkedIn is the #1 entity now ... but all things have a life cycle. Today's giant is tomorrow's buggy whip. Be aware of up and coming social media sites, especially if they have to do with job search (even after you get your next job!).

Google has entered the job aggregation world. I suggest using this giant to your best advantage. I just joined a site called joivy.com, where I've established the HIRED! Job Search community. And Snapchat, according to Peter Pones, is an excellent place to "stalk" potential employers (and it's not just for teenagers). He suggests taking advantage of the site's tutorials, network, telling a story through video clips, comments and pictures (where have I heard this advice before?).[33]

Set-up for all the other social media sites is basically the same as what we went through for LinkedIn and, more importantly, your content should be the same or close to it. I can't tell you how many times I've heard Recruiters tell me they bounced a candidate when his/her resume and profiles were not even close to being the same. Populate your sites of choice with the same content you created for LinkedIn. Don't make yourself crazy!

Keep in mind that Recruiters look at other social media sites as much to eliminate candidates as to qualify them. This is why I shy away from Facebook and Twitter. By pressing **Send**, the rest of the world has access to content you may, later, regret posting. One story of this I often tell is about a beloved professor at a small college who took a vacation to the Florida gulf coast (the Redneck Riviera"), was enjoying an adult beverage when someone took his photo, drink in hand. The photograph was posted on a Facebook account. The president of the college somehow was made aware of the posting and immediately fired the man for a violation of the school's morals clause. Nothing illegal was committed; the professor wasn't on campus or at a college function, but he lost his job because of a social media posting. Stay professional even though it's boring. Big Brother is watching, so beware!

"Social Media is an amazing tool,
but it's really face-to-face interaction
that makes a long-term impact."
-Felicia Day

[33] Peter Jones, 5 Ways to Use Snapchat in your Job Search, The Job Search Network.

Chapter 7: Putting It All Together

"Manufacturing is more than just putting parts together. It's coming up with ideas, testing principles and perfecting the engineering, as well as final assembly."
-James Dyson

You've gathered all the parts to build a successful Marketing Campaign. I've shared the ideas and tested its principals on similar candidates over many years in a changing job search landscape in an attempt to perfect the engineering. Now's the time for final assembly. Are you ready to be employed? I know you've been chomping at the bit, so let's start with your new resume.

Richard Morgan is an executive and outplacement counselor, a certified resume writer, a branding expert, a long-time job networking volunteer, a shoulder to lean on for those in job transition, and so much more. He also has the same wacky sense of humor as me. More than anything else, Richard is a close, trusted friend. Many elements of this chapter were written by my buddy Richard Morgan. Enjoy!

The Wonderful World of Resumes

It's amazing how the "least popular" element of the modern job search campaign is one of the most critical. That's right, it's the wonderful world of resumes (pause here for loud, frightening background music!!). As a certified resume writer and professional coach, I have encountered hundreds of these documents spanning virtually every category and industry sector. No matter the experience or confidence level, there are several points about the resume common to nearly every professional in transition. Do any of these sound familiar?

- Uncertain or afraid what others will think of your resume?
- Never quite satisfied with the document, often keeping it in a stage of "perpetual change?"
- Are you focusing almost exclusively on events of the past, making it only a historical document?
- Not sure how to build a resume and what elements are important to your target audience?
- Are you following the advice of others specific to the resume design and content, which may be a problem if those influences do not have experience in creating the content to help in a career campaign?

Misses of Resume Writing

To ensure hitting the mark with your resume, you must know your target. What is interesting is that the identification of your target begins with knowing what or where you may be "off the mark." I like to call these items the items the "m*isses"* of resume writing*:*

1. ***Misdirection*** - Essentially, information that takes you in the wrong direction, such as details, ideas, or guidance that may not be accurate because the primary purpose is to capture historic career data only (i.e., titles no longer used). Therefore, each professional following a path of misdirection, is headed down the same path that has not or will not lead to desired results.
2. ***Misunderstanding*** - Hearing ideas that in theory may be good; yet, you are not sure what they mean or how to best use them for yourself. This level of misunderstanding often leads to the creation of answers to critical resume questions without knowing

the impact such answers will add to one's perceived value by key decision makers in the hiring process.

3. ***Misinformed*** - Plain old info that is circulating out there but just ain't so (see: The White Space Myth below). What is amazing is many of these concepts are still regarded as the right methods and measures within the world of resume development and are therefore perpetuated as iconic solutions. A personal favorite of mine, by the way, is "all you need is a one-page resume"!

With all the information available to jobseekers through the internet, word of mouth, and pseudo-experts, it is no surprise that one of the biggest questions on the minds of those in transition would be, "*What is the right approach to building a resume?"* Guess what, I have a good answer to this and many related questions surrounding what has become the initial step and greatest hurdle for those in transition when it comes to developing their professional marketing content and agenda - having the best possible resume!

What's on the menu?

In a restaurant, you are provided with a menu to select the items you prefer to eat; in other words, what works best for you. Like a menu with many pages and selections to choose from, maneuvering through the immense information out there on the right approach to constructing your resume may take a while. In addition, chances are, you may see someone walking by with a different "selection" and wish that this is what you had ordered.

So, are we talking about dinner choices or resumes here?

Both! If you order from a large menu, you will likely see the server walk by with something you did not order and say to yourself, "that's what I should have gone with!" It doesn't mean you made a bad decision. You are simply questioning if your decision was the right one. In the end, you must be happy with your choice! When listening to the opinions and influences regarding your resume, the same is true. If you follow the advice in this chapter, it will guide you through a logical and well-explained approach to developing a resume model that serves your career campaign needs. To say I have the answer to a perfect resume would be a bold statement. Instead, my goal is to share an approach whereby you can capture and cultivate the details necessary to convey your brand effectively to others. Not to oversimplify, but, in the end, it is the provision of that information that will allow you to demonstrate skills, diversity, and your ability to add value to those organizations you wish to target.

What's your shoe size? (Resume Choices)

Anyone who has shopped for shoes knows one size does not fit all. The same is true with resumes. No single model fits perfectly for every candidate. The same is true in creating a resume. There's more than one type and you should be made aware of them to choose which style is the right fit for your needs.

The most widely used resumes fall into three categories: Chronological, Functional, and Hybrid.

Chronological:

The most widely used resume model is the Chronological, whereby the candidate's work history is captured in reverse order (from when the Dead Sea only had the sniffles through your most recent position). It is preferred by most professionals who construct their own resume because it follows their work history timeline, focusing mainly upon tasks, defined roles, and the elements of the past employers and companies.

Functional:

The functional approach is used for many reasons, primarily to bring focus on one's skills as opposed to a chronological timeline. The skills and accomplishments are highlighted at the beginning of the resume, with a short section that captures the work history (often not in chronological order or with dates), then education and professional training at the end. Often, this model is used by professionals trying to shed light on the skills associated with specialized fields or roles. In addition, this model is used by candidates wanting to "deflect" focus from the chronological elements of the resume. These reasons include limited experience or skills in an area, gaps in employment, or employment at several different companies. The primary downside to such a resume is that it may been seen by hiring team decision makers as a device for concealing experience versus clearly conveying relevant experience.

Hybrid *(Blended or Combination):*
Gosh, combination platters appear to be popular in restaurants, or when selecting the options for your cable TV or cell phone services. These blended packages are a great way to capture many elements. The same is true of the Hybrid Resume, whereby the reader will get a snapshot of the professional's "headline," summary of qualifications and skills, relevant work history, and key achievements.

Without question, this model has become the most popular resume model for those making hiring decisions because of the type and position of the information presented. The greatest downsize to such a resume is it requires skill and patience generating the combination platform (how to provide the right information without capturing too much detail).

Much more on Hybrid Resumes later in this chapter.

Other Resume Types include:

Infographic - The first time I saw an infographic resume I thought I was having an "acid flash-forward" (flash forward because I never dropped acid, so it would be impossible to have an acid flashback). This style resume is full of graphics, colors, charts, and anything else possible, including the kitchen sink.

If you take your chances with an infographic, it should go only to a Hiring Manager, never to HR because they won't know what to do with it. An infographic resume cannot get through an ATS. The only people who I can see being successful with an infographic resume's use would be people in the graphic arts and marketing.

Video - If you're comfortable in front of a camera (and can read a script) you might want to add a video of some sort to your Marketing Campaign in addition to a paper resume. If done right, you can present yourself to your audience for it to "see you" as more than just another piece of paper in the queue. You become human.

How do I make a video of myself?

They are relatively easy to produce. If you have a camera (your phone would work), a computer, and a slide advancer, you're pretty well set. The trick is to place the camera on your computer such that you're "looking through' the lens without moving your eyes.

Get started by creating a PowerPoint of what you want to say and use your computer screen as a teleprompter. A cheap slide advancer allows you to read your script (use large font size so you can read your script). Remember to rehearse so you don't sound like you are reading. Check for adequate lighting and let your personality shine through.

This same method can be used to present your Value Proposition deck. Either or both can be uploaded to YouTube, then linked to your LinkedIn profile. They can also be uploaded onto QR codes and added to your business card. No one else will take this tact, so you will immediately differentiate yourself from other candidates. Have some fun while you're at it!

Curriculum Vitae (C/V) - Generally not used in the United States, a C/V is longer and more involved than a conventional resume. Those in academics typically need a C/V to include courses, publications, whitepapers, etc.

Government - If you thought a C/V was long, resumes for governmental positions would embarrass Herman Melville and William Faulkner. Whereas most resumes should be limited to two pages, government resumes can extend beyond a dozen without breathing hard.

Unicorns & Other (Resume) Myths

To dream is good, but to believe in things that just aren't real is something very different. Unicorns are mythical creatures and being a fan of these flying horses brings excitement to many while causing no harm. Myths and bad information regarding resumes are a different story.

When working with a client, I try to share the best approach to each step in his/her search agenda (including the resume) along with reasons why these approaches are worthy of consideration. More times than not, when I ask what questions the candidate has when beginning the process, the subject of resumes is always at the top of the list.

Because the resume is such a critical item, let's travel down the road of myths, bad ideas, and "it just ain't so" items specific to the resume:

Myth 1. You should have only 1 page:

Not true. With the current reliance on Applicant Tracking System (ATS) software packages and the importance placed on keywords, having a 1-page resume is a recipe for disaster

Myth 2. Start with an "objective" section:

Objectives are currently seen as passé. If you have a resume, chances are they know what your objective is! Better than an objective is simply stating the job title you seek. (Besides, it's another set of Keywords!)

Myth 3. Experience - only go back 10 years:

Focus on all experience that shows your value, which may take the reader back further than 10 years or your last few roles. Ten years is only a rule of thumb, not one of the Ten Commandments.

Myth 4. Use catchy terms like "highly motivated," "successful," "loyal," "team-player," "dedicated," etc.

This "real estate" is far too valuable and shouldn't be wasted.

Myth 5. Always make it fancy to standout with creative design:

Not a good idea. Such designs can halt the ATS and cast you into the Black Hole.

Myth 6. Revise your resume to each job you apply for:

Not a smart idea despite what virtually all the pundits will tell you. Your experience and skills are as they are and you must be innovative, capturing the important details of your professional value and potential in multiple organizations. That said, if you are scripting your resume to fit each job, how can you keep up with all the different resumes? Besides, if you take things out, the odds are great that you'll forget to put some back.

Instead, you should have discovered and loaded most of the keywords for your job title in the "Words-to-Work" process. (BIG hint: Find it in the cover letter subchapter!)

Myth 7. Fill white space with keywords in white print: *Don't believe it! The "White Space Myth" has been floated around for years and it's totally bogus! Recruiters can do a document search for keywords and everywhere you put a word in white type, it will show up as a yellow blotch. Don't believe me? Give it* *a try. Recruiters figure, "Scam us now, scam us later," your chances are over.*

Keyword Makeover?

Yes, but not just as space fillers (passionate, hard-working, dedicated, team-player, over-achiever, results-oriented, etc.). Suggestion: Utilize this valuable real estate by capturing your skills, capabilities (defined role), and your achievements. The art of keywords is one that cannot be overstated, AI devoted the entire chapter to them!

At this point in your career campaign, it is important to be aware of what keywords are important to the remainder of the marketplace. The terminology you used in the past may not be what is generally valued in the modern work environment. This does not mean you don't know what you are talking about, nor do I mean to indicate you have no idea how to convey your brand identity. Instead, you may simply require a bit of a "key word makeover!" A tour through current job openings and LinkedIn terminology of similar professionals may prove an "eye-opener"! Let me offer this example:

Your resume contains the words "Sales" and "Nationwide Sales Rep" in multiple places. In fact, these terms were the position titles offered by the companies where you held those roles. Today, the words "Sales" and "Nationwide Sales Rep" may have been replaced by "Business Development" or "National Key Account Manager." While it may seem a minor point, these are the words being used by Recruiters, HR managers, and as guidepost filters in Applicant Tracking Systems. Therefore, would it make sense to use the antiquated terminology of yesteryear, or should you use the verbiage that aligns your skills and brand to the needs of current search teams? (Gets you found.)

Construction of a Hybrid Resume

1. *Contact Information*

   Many start the resume with highly creative opening sections that contain their contact details. This opening section should contain the primary contact/ identification details for the reader to use in reaching out to the candidate. Ultimately, the person should provide his/her name (larger font than the other information in this section), the metro or regional area in which the candidate resides, phone number, email address, and LinkedIn URL.

There are a few things to avoid within this section:

- No lines, inserted content, nor multiple columns (I recommend centered information with a 10-12pt space between this information and the headline/summary section.
- No mixture of all upper-case words and font types.
- No street address, if the company wants your contact details above what is on the resume, they will request an advanced application as the hiring process continues.
- Do not use words like "Phone" or "Email" or Linkedin address. This is "old school," besides, the reader will be able to tell that the information provided is your phone, email, etc.

Other things to be aware of:

- Some people add their title immediately under their contact information. (Al recommends this)
- Erase underlines and different color fonts that may appear under your email or LinkedIn addresses (keep everything consistent with other information in the top section of the resume).

John Smith

Greater Boston Area, 02018 john.smith@gmail.com
770-555-3210 www.LinkedIn/in/JohnSmith

Operations Manager

2. *Tagline / Headline / Summary / Value Proposition* (Replaces the old "objective" section)

Example – Headline and Summary / Value Proposition

HR Executive – Operations Management | Training & Development | Talent Acquisition
Possessing more than 15 years of experience in diverse industries including banking, international logistics, and manufacturing. Leveraging inherent skills to manage successful business operations, identify/mitigate risk, direct projects, manage human resources, and/or deliver brand enhancement through a Value Proposition or Select Accomplishments section.

Note: The Value Proposition is the opportunity to demonstrate what you're qualified to do – ultimately, what you can do for the company.

3. *Core Competencies or Skills*

Core competencies can be used to gain the interest of the person reading your resume. The skills you highlight support the primary message of the resume, "Here are my skills and I will bring them with me once hired as part of your company!" Your top skills may or may not be evident to the average person reading your resume. Therefore, it is essential that these core skills are captured rather than left to chance. Those key skill items are going to be represented again within the content of your resume as part of your defined role, achievements and/or success stories. Here's an example of core competencies or key skills:

Strategic Relationship Building	Training/Development
Process Improvement	Regional Management
Budget Design/Adherence	Cost Control

A word of advice when creating this list of skills: make sure these are terms that define your professional value rather than knowledge within a technology or industry specific sector. In other words, expertise in Excel or Salesforce brings merit to any applicant; but, these are considered acquired technologies versus inherent skills that define the professional. Therefore, these items would be captured in another section of the resume.

4. *Professional Experience*

It is this section that often provides the best snapshot into the qualifications of each professional based upon experience in the workplace. The main thing to remember is that the purpose of this information should not be to merely capture one's professional past. Instead, the goal should be to demonstrate value within the environment of the potential company based upon a combined presentation of the following elements:

- *Company name, city, state, dates of employment*
- *Title or position (typically in bold font)*
- *Description and summary of role and areas of accountability*
- *Achievements or accomplishments*

The presentation of a defined role summary and achievement items define the "Blended Resume" (hybrid) model. Add to this the fact that this format promotes the utilization of keywords and further increases the searchability factor of the candidate when resumes are sent electronically or applied to an ATS (Applicant Tracking System). The following is an example of professional experience items presented within a resume:

Secure Financial Corporation - Columbus, IN

Director of Operational Efficiency (2013 - 2015)

Executed corporate efficiency initiatives, as well as the identification and analysis of structural and process improvement opportunities. Led team of direct and indirect reports from a cross-functional team representing finance,

HR, and operations targeting positive change initiatives to impact entire organization.

Achievement(s):

- Achieved $6MM expense reduction, significantly improving efficiency ratio by assessing expense policies and approval system, establishing new corporate expense agenda;
- Earned "President's Award for Innovative Contribution."

5. *Additional Experience*

This is not a section needed for each professional constructing a resume. For most, however, this section can offer the reader a deeper dive into their platform of experience without some of the negative derivatives often associated with employment history from a certain period within our career. To be frank, one of the greatest fears facing professionals in career transition who have some level of maturity on their side is a bad word that has but three letters - **AGE!** More than any other concern I hear from professionals I coach, their fear of how age may be "stacked" against them and, based upon the way they market their brand, this may be a legitimate fear!

If we align with one of the initial premises, which is to create brand identity, then the best way to share the width of your river of experience versus showing how deep the water runs is to use an "Additional Experience" section. In this section, you can illustrate the following without the negative impact elements:

- Diversity of experience across different firms or industries
- Progression of roles within one's career
- Chance to share involvement in unique and "skills development and growth" roles.
- You can show more experience in a section in which dates are not captured.

Here is a brief example of an experience item that could appear in the Additional Experience section:

Project Manager - Total System Services, Inc.
Managed comprehensive operation program tasks to include technology research, product and supplier evaluations, senior management recommendations, facilitating software development implementations, and delivery of all training.

6. *Education / Training / Professional Development / Certifications / Awards*

It is within this section that one can capture the items that align them with others, while, offering a degree of separation based upon meritorious performance and exceptional work/life experiences. In other words, the degree-of-separation items can be captured in this section of the resume along with those elements that add value to your professional persona, but do not fit comfortably in other sections. Here are the primary components:

- **College Degree** – Degree type, concentration, university or college name (GPA may be added for some professions);
- **Training:** If training adds Brand "credibility";
- **Certifications**: If current or adds value (Lotus 123 won't);
- **Awards**: Confirm/demonstrate skills;
- **Special Organizations/Volunteer:** Especially when you hold a position of influence or clearly depict professional skills to add value to that organization or entity.

Below is an example of how this section could appear:

Education · Professional Development · Awards

Bachelor of Arts, Speech Communications
Appalachian State University

Executive Training Program - The Leadership Institute (Synovus)
Senior Human Resources Certification (SPHR)
Certified MBTI Facilitator
Examiner, Malcolm Baldrige National Quality Award
Vice President/Treasurer - The Helping Hand Organization

Although different in a few instances from Richard's resume described above, below is an example of what Al's Hybrid resume looks like. There are two versions, the first is formatted for electronic submissions and the second is to hand to a real, live human being in your interview. Al's E-Resume example:

Jill Schmill

Atlanta, GA 30022 Jillschmill@icloud.com
(678) 555-6286 https://www.linkedin.com/in/jillschmillatl

Enterprise & Cloud (SaaS) Sales Executive

Career Summary

Top 20 Global Enterprise Sales Executive Profiles - LinkedIn. Multiple award-winning sales executive with a proven ability to develop and execute innovative plans with strategic vision to creatively enhance market share and annual profits. Turns untapped and unprofitable territories into positive revenue producers.

Value Proposition

Key Accomplishments	Sales & Management Awards	Tech Platforms
$16.47 million Team Pipeline	New Client Sales (2012 & 2013)	SaaS & Cloud
$6.12 million Personal Pipeline	Sales Excellence Club (2011)	SalesForce.com
67% Revenue Increase	N Squard Club (2006-2009)	Mobile App.
$42.3 million qualified pipeline	Regional Mgr Diamond Sales Club (2000-2005)	
$934,783 (From Zero) in 12 months	Sales Rep Karat Sales Club (1996-1999)	
Establishing new regional sales office	Net New Business & Talent Management Growth	

Professional Experience

MyEmployees, Castle Hayne, NC 2016 – Present
Business Engagement Cloud Sales Executive, National

Mobile app & Cloud (SaaS) software platform, deliver C-Level, senior managers & all stakeholders the technology providing insight into talent management, succession, engagement, and on-boarding. Hand-picked by CEO and Executive team to create an enterprise sales team and strategy to sell the MyEmployees solution to C-level and Executive level prospects at the global corporate office.

- Built a team pipeline of $16.47 million in 8 months with 2 industry novice sales reps, including a personal pipeline of $6.12 million. On track to increase annual revenue by 67%.
- Developed, executed and trained enterprise team on an executive level complex solutions sales process specific to prospect business challenges.
- Design and train sales presentation methodology to drive C-suite initiatives & articulate expected ROI.

Globoforce, Southborough, MA 2014 – 2016
Global Enterprise SaaS Sales Executive, Southeast USA

Al's Interview Resume:

Jill Schmill

Atlanta, GA 30022 Jillschmill@icloud.com

(678) 555-6286 https://www.linkedin.com/in/jillschmillatl

Enterprise & Cloud (SaaS) Sales Executive

Career Summary

Top 20 Global Enterprise Sales Executive Profiles - LinkedIn. Multiple award-winning sales executive with a proven ability to develop and execute innovative plans with strategic vision to creatively enhance market share and annual profits. Turns untapped and unprofitable territories into positive revenue producers.

Value Proposition

Key Accomplishments	Sales & Management Awards	Tech Platforms
• $16.47 million Team Pipeline	New Client Sales (2012 & 2013)	SaaS
• $6.12 million Personal Pipeline	Sales Excellence Club (2011)	SalesForce.com
• 67% Revenue Increase	N Squared Club (2006-2009)	Mobile App.
• $42.3 million qualified pipeline	Regional Mgr. Diamond Sales Club (2000-2005)	Cloud
• $934,783 (From Zero) in 12 months	Sales Rep Karat Sales Club (1996-1999)	
• Establishing new regional sales office	Net New Business & Talent Management Growth	

Professional Experience

MyEmployees, Castle Hayne, NC 2016 – Present

Business Engagement Cloud Sales Executive, National

Mobile app & Cloud (SaaS) software platform, deliver C-Level, senior managers & all stakeholders the technology providing insight into talent management, succession, engagement, and on-boarding. Hand-picked by CEO and Executive team to create an enterprise sales team and strategy to sell the MyEmployees solution to C-level and Executive level prospects at the global corporate office.

- Built a team pipeline of $16.47 million in 8 months with 2 industry novice sales reps, including a personal pipeline of $6.12 million. On track to increase annual revenue by 67%.
- Developed, executed and trained enterprise team on an executive level complex solutions sales process specific to prospect business challenges.
- Design and train sales presentation methodology to drive C-suite initiatives & articulate expected ROI.

Globoforce, Southborough, MA 2014 – 2016

Global Enterprise SaaS Sales Executive, Southeast USA

It's important to note the formatting differences and why. Some Applicant Tracking System software packages can't "read" your resume if the formatting isn't recognized. What's worse, they don't all work the same, so I recommend you avoid any problems by formatting your e-resume devoid of the possible sticking points. Things that can make an ATS "blow-up" include:

- Use of the Header/Footer function (including page numbers),
- Dividing lines,
- Borders,
- Use of the table or column function,
- Graphics (i. e., pictures, symbols, or a QR code),
- Text boxes

Note: "Quick & Dirty" recommended resume choices:

Action Item	Recommendation
Resume Style	Hybrid
Font Type	Arial, Calibri, Cambria, Times New Roman (these 4 only!)
Font Size(s)	Headings: 14 (16 name) Body: 10-12
Save As	.doc/.docx, .pdf, .txt (Send .doc/.docx unless otherwise specified)
Save As (Title)	Name, Name1, Name.1, Name0.1, NameYear, NameTitle, NameResume,
Do Nots	ResumeName Name & number other than 1
Never	Never Lie!

Value Proposition (resume)

Everyone has a different take on resumes and it's certainly the case here. Whereas I agree with Richard Morgan on every point above, how I create some of those elements varies a bit. It's your choice which one works for you.

It's said that a Recruiter can "read" a resume in 2-6 seconds. Imagine, your entire professional career summed-up in 6 seconds or less! Think about it, if you don't have something to grab a reader's attention from the get-go, it doesn't matter if you're better than sliced bread, you don't have a chance of getting an interview much less a job. So, I like including something in the top half of the resume's first page as a showstopper. I call it a Value Proposition (or Select Accomplishments).

Ideally, a Value Proposition is 1-3 columns across the page with headings and 3-6 examples under each heading. These are the things that you bring to the table for your prospective employer. They allow a Hiring Manager quickly to review the reasons you should be the choice without scouring multiple paragraphs. Although some Recruiters frown on both a Hybrid resume and its Value Proposition, trust me when I tell you every Hiring Manager will love it!

What goes in a Value Proposition?

In short, your value to a company; those things that set you apart from other candidates such as awards, languages, advanced degrees, publications, numbers, dollars or percentages, computer skills, software, etc. Remember all those accomplishments and skills you uncovered earlier? Those are among the things you should bring to the attention of Hiring Managers in your Value Proposition section. What's more, most of the words and phrases used will be the keywords Recruiters are seeking.

One last thing to keep in mind: Every claim you make in your Value Proposition needs to be reiterated in the body of your resume as a third-party proof of where and when they were accomplished. It's all the other candidates who lie ... not you!

It's not just Richard and me recommending a Hybrid Resume. Alan Carniol, founder of Interview Success, agrees as well. "If you're worried about being screened out by HR because of your experience, here are three simple steps you can take to "age-proof" your resume:

1. Don't list jobs from more than 15-20 years ago.
2. Leave off graduation dates.

3. Consider using a "combination resume" (Hybrid). This is a special type of resume layout where you communicate your key skills and experiences before you detail your work history.
4. Apply for jobs through the "side door" where Hiring Managers will take a liking to you and decide they want you on their team before ever seeing your resume. You won't have to contend with institutional ageism and get an opportunity to demonstrate your value."

How do I?

Q: *How do I cover "gaps" in employment?*
A: First, don't include months, use only years. This gives you some fudge factor without lying. A resume is NOT an application.

Q: *How do I decide which resume version to send to a Hiring Manager?*
A: One resume - problem solved! The only thing you should ever change is the title at the top of the page to match the title in the job description.

Q: *I have heard that the resume should match the job description, true or not?*
A: Yes and No. Let me explain: After going through the "Words-to-Work" process, you should have discovered most of the keywords used in your job title's descriptions. A unique cover letter should take care of the rest (see Cover Letter section later in the next subchapter)

Q: *How can I use my resume to show my skills in areas other than in my last job(s)?*
A: Research market and check your competition!

Rules to Keeping the Train Rolling

1. Don't send your resume to dozens of jobs each week

2. You do not need lots of versions of your resume.
3. Watch the inserts, lines, headers, and footers because these can stop you getting through the ATS
4. Never send your resume to "To whom it may concern." Every resume should be accompanied by a "letter of introduction."

Cover-Up, You're Indecent!

My chief goal for this book (and my previous) is to show readers *every path to employment in the social media era*. There was one glaring piece missing in the previous book: Not a word about cover letters. The reasoning was valid; not a single Recruiter I'd asked during the previous five or six years said they ever read a cover letter unless the position required extensive writing skills. Now's my opportunity to right that wrong, but not for the reasons you might suspect.

For the most part, no HUMAN reader will ever read your cover letter, but the ATS will. The goal for your cover letter should be to satisfy the ATSs' "Rule of Three" so you get through the Black Hole when you apply online for posted jobs.

Here's how we will do it: Your cover letter will be the third page of your resume when you upload for online submissions.

Covers have to go on top!

Who says? I don't know about you, but my bed has covers above me and below me. Do you sleep on your mattress? Yuck! Allow me to explain before you call the friendly people handling the white jackets with long sleeves.

Applicant Tracking Systems scan the document you upload to fill in its little boxes (previous employers, education, etc.) searching all the while for specific keywords. The cover letter is added to your resume to enhance the number of job-specific keywords, thus satisfying the Rule of Three and allowing you a better chance to escape the Black Hole without you changing the resume itself. But it needs to be the document's third page because the ATS would populate its boxes with the wrong information if the cover is page one. That would open up an entirely different can of worms!

We will accomplish this feat by using the "T-Format Cover Letter." This is a one-page document and 1-page only. Let's start from the beginning:

1. **Heading** – Use the exact same heading as on your resume (remember NOT to use the header/footer function because some ATSs can reject submissions that include that feature).
2. **Title** – On the first line below the heading, include the following: **Re: Job Title**. Use the exact wording as in the job description. The title is another set of keywords!
3. **Requisition Number** – If the job description has a requisition number (aka Job I.D. Number) you should enter the following: **Req. #: __________**.

(**Note:** When networking into a company, including these will make it easier for your submission to be found, "Hi, Jane. I have applied to <u>This Position</u>, <u>Job ID Number</u>. Would you mind pulling my submission out of the queue to get to the Recruiter because ..."

4. **Top of the T** – Add a three-line, keyword-rich comment why you are perfect for this job ending with: Here are a few examples:
5. **Columns** – You will create two columns (without using the column feature (remember using the column or table feature can stop you in your tracks when applying online).
   a. On the left side, take a word or phrase from the job description (all keywords!) to enter at the left margin (The word or phrase will be a skill, requirement, or preferred quality) then tab over to create a column

b. On the right side, you will show how you meet or exceed what they require or prefer.

(**Note:** If a company asks for 5 years' experience and you have 10, enter 5+ years' experience. Continue adding requirements, etc., you believe are most important. Seven or so should do the trick.)

6. **Ending** – Type: Looking forward to speaking with you, Sincerely, YOUR NAME
7. **Save** – Save this document (e.g., XYZ Corp. Cover)
8. **Copy** – Copy this entire document
9. **Open** – Open your resume document
10. **Paste** – Paste this as the third (or last) page of your resume
11. **Save** – Save your resume with the cover letter as the third page
12. **Upload** – Upload this 3-page document (resume with cover letter)
13. **Cover Letter** – If prompted to upload a cover letter, upload the same cover letter!

(**Note:** If you have used this tactic, remember to delete the previous cover letter from the resume document).

As I've said before, I didn't write the rulebook, I just read it and want you to take full advantage of the crazy game they created.

Letter of Introduction

If the goal of your cover letter is to get your resume through the ATS and into the hands of a TAM, a Letter of Introduction is to avoid the Black Hole entirely, so your resume is read by someone with two eyes and a brain from the get-go.

Your Letter of Introduction should be addressed to a specific person, and the higher up the executive totem pole the better. In my opinion, this is a top-down tactic. You want the target executive to direct people below him/her to take action on your behalf.

Construction is similar to that of a cover letter, except your letter of introduction should be more formal. If you have personalized stationary, use it. If not, I recommend its creation. It's dated and addressed to the executive, including title and with the company's address. The body should include a 3-5-line paragraph why your resume should be read followed by examples of what you bring to the table. Conclude with a brief paragraph formally asking for a meeting. Attach your resume.

JobScan

There's an interesting tool you should consider using, but only judiciously. It's called Jobscan.co. (**Note:** This is not a typo, it's dot co, not dot com.)

JobScan.co allows you to upload your resume and the job description you want to apply for, then reads your submission and, using its proprietary algorithm, scores your resume versus the job description. I have clients use this tool first with their resume only then again with their cover letter added as the third page. When they score 85% or above, I tell them, "Let it fly."

There's one catch to JobScan.co you should keep in mind: you only get 5 bites at the apple per month before it charges you (this could change if it gets wind of this subchapter). If it charged a few bucks for each submission (each bite at the apple), I would give my full backing for its use, but I believe the monthly fee is too high. Of course, it didn't ask my opinion.

Other, similar companies are certain to crop up with increasing frequency (and accuracy, with any luck). VMock.com is the most recent one to cross my desk (Thanks Mike Hydzik). At least for now, this site only gives you one chance before charging.

Give it a try, determine if its conclusions are valid and use these tools to your best advantage!

Personal Website

"If you're trying to land a new job this year, a personal website could be your secret weapon," writes Jacqueline Smith in her Business Insider article, "Here's Why Every Job Seeker Needs a Personal Website - And What It Should Include." The argument is that a personal website is the best method for creating and maintaining your personal brand.[34]

Now, I'm all for Personal Branding and carrying it throughout your Marketing Campaign. I can clearly see the usefulness of a personal website for web designers, those in the graphic arts, marketing, and many similar jobs, but I question the necessity of a personal website for the average job seeker.

Out of curiosity, I conducted an unscientific poll on LinkedIn. In it I asked the following two questions:

- How important is a personal website to your recruiting world and personal experience as a Recruiter?
- What percentage (rough number) of candidates were chosen because of their personal website?

Results: Comments were as opposite as possible. Either the respondents were gung-ho for or totally against personal websites. Here are a couple examples (Quotes limited to Recruiters):

"Anything a candidate can do to stand out and rise above will benefit them greatly. A website is a way to control the content about you in cyberspace. And it is only $10.00 for the year to do

---

[34] Jacquelyn Smith, Here's Why Every Job Seeker needs a Personal Website - and What It Should include, *Business Insider*, Jan. 14, 2015.

so. Crazy if you don't do it. If the choice is between two candidates, one has a website, the other does not. The website one will win 100% of the time."

-Dan Jourdan

"Unless you're a web developer, UI developer. etc., I don't think a personal website is going to help you."

-Patrick Jeter

"Personally, I do not believe your personal website will get you a job, but it can sure COST you one."

-Jon Ferns

Natasa Djukanovic, a spokesperson for the .ME Registry says, "We have found in our research that a website gives the option to be creative and show personality, which is important because it drives attention," then adds, "An ordinary LinkedIn account doesn't give too much liberty, or any options at all, to [stand out] from the crowd."[35] Whereas I agree that candidates should showcase their creativity, unique brand and personality, I beg to differ regarding LinkedIn.

Every client of mine has a Value Proposition deck in his/her Intro section (formerly Heading and Summary). Additionally, LinkedIn allows members to upload PowerPoint or SlideShares, links to videos, projects, recommendations, and countless other devices to differentiate yourself from your competition.

We know from a 2012 jobvite.com survey that 93% of Recruiters use LinkedIn as their primary search tool, but I can't

---

[35] Jacquelyn Smith, Here's Why Every Job Seeker needs a Personal Website - and What It Should include, *Business Insider*, January 14, 2015.

seem to find statistics to back up the claims that a personal website is a *necessity.*

All that being said, if you believe a personal website will set you apart from other candidates AND you have the time and ability to keep your website up to date, I'm all for it. If you decide a personal website is for you, I recommend the advice of Dan Schawbel of workplacetrends.com, who says your website should contain the following:[36]

- An Introduction
- Your Bio
- Work Experience (or resume)
- Education
- Projects or samples of your work
- Skills
- An Image Gallery
- Testimonials or references
- Videos
- Professional recognition, and
- Social Elements

One final question: Now that you have your personal website, how are you going to drive Recruiters and others to it?

Marketing Brochures

You know those slick sales brochures you see everywhere about products from menu items to exotic resorts? You should consider using any of the various forms of Marketing Brochure (both paper and electronic) as a part of your campaign. There are as many types as there are uses. If for no other reason,

---

[36] Jacquelyn Smith, Here's Why Every Job Seeker needs a Personal Website - and What It Should include, *Business Insider*, January 14, 2015.

Marketing Brochures should set you apart from other candidates and demonstrate your creativity.

In some cases, Marketing Brochures can be more effective than a resume – if you can find the right person or people to send it to (and follow-up with). Certainly, people with a large gap in their professional history and those changing professions should utilize Marketing Brochures as a networking and job search tool. They tell your story in a manner resumes cannot. Marketing Brochures tell a story.

A **Background** brochure can introduce you to someone who knows nothing about you. Your Background Brochure can be used in an initial interview, as well. It's my opinion that every candidate should have a Brochure of some type for Final Interviews. I call mine a **Seal-the-Deal** brochure. Jay Litton, who runs the largest church-based Job Networking group (at Roswell United Methodist Church) north of Atlanta has what he calls "The WOW! Interview."[37] He uses a flip chart to present the material (See Jay's subchapter in the interview chapter and/or check it out at wowinterview.com)

Marketing Brochure types:

- Tri-fold - 1 sheet of paper (usually some sort of card stock or slick paper), using landscape orientation with three columns. creating a six-paneled document folded in thirds
- Rack Card - 2-sided document, created from ⅓ of one sheet of cardstock (created like a Tri-fold)
- Bi-Fold - 1 sheet of paper, landscape orientation with two columns creating a 4-paneled document folded in the center

---

[37] wowinterview.com

- Multi-fold - Similar to Bi-fold in construction, using 2 sheets (or more) creating an 8-page center-folded and stapled booklet
- Portfolio - For executives and those in the graphic arts, is a multi-page bound booklet.
- Flip Chart - Multiple landscape oriented pages spiral bound in a presentation format
- PowerPoint or Slideshare

Marketing Brochures should be sent through the mail or by a delivery service, but never electronically because the formatting would be ruined; besides, since people get so little mail now, people read more of the mail they get. Here's an example:

> Many years ago, a client was trying to become a store manager for one of the largest retailers in the country, found the company had a regional office in his town, and mailed one of his Marketing Brochures to the Regional President. He anticipated its arrival on a Friday and called the Regional President's office. He reached her admin. He explained what he had done and asked if she had seen the document. The admin said she hadn't, but the mail had just arrived. She put my client on hold to look, but was back within seconds saying, "It's not here, but I'll look for it Monday." Thinking quickly, the client said, "That was fast, how many pieces of mail does she get in an average day?" The reply was only about four! Imagine how many unsolicited emails she gets and what she does with them.

I don't know about you, but most emails I get from people I don't know go immediately into my trash bin, DELETE!

The key to your success with a Background Marketing Brochure is to follow-up soon after the piece should arrive. Pick up the phone and call. Calling before business normally starts, at lunch-time or after 5:00 PM local time increases your chances of the target person picking up the phone.

Executive Assistants can help you or stop you in your tracks. Try making nice with them, but never lie! Most of them open virtually all the executive's mail and have a keen eye for important and interesting information. They also have built-in bull$#!+ alarms. They can make certain your material gets to the executive or never does.

Note: Only about 20% of your Marketing Brochures will reach your target executive and you will be rebuffed often. Keep plugging away. You only need one job.

Value Proposition decks

If resumes can be read in 2-6 seconds, the same time frame can be assumed for a LinkedIn profile.

The "Words-to-Work" process, if done correctly (job title is in demand and your profile is properly optimized), should attract more profile views by Recruiters and TAMs than you could possibly expect otherwise. The object from this point on is to give them a reason(s) to stay on your profile longer than normal. You want to suck all the oxygen out of the room. This is where uploading a Value Proposition deck can help.

Similar to, but more involved than Marketing Brochures, a Value Proposition is designed to show-off what you bring to the table with more panache than a resume ever could. They are relatively easy to create and are limited only by your imagination.

To get started, open PowerPoint and choose a template that appeals to you. I prefer more simple templates because it's the content you want people to note, not the background. My recommendation is to try to have a background that is somehow related to your industry or title. If none of the PowerPoint templates appeal, do an internet search for other available templates.

What do I put in my Value Proposition?

Good question. Not to be a smart aleck, but only you can properly answer this question. Here are a few ideas for inclusion:

- **Title Page** should have your name, a picture, desired job title(s) and the term: Value Proposition. For consistency, I suggest using the same picture as your LinkedIn profile.
- **Concluding Page**: This is where I like to come full circle with your name, job title(s), and contact information. Never take for granted someone's level of intelligence!

Wait a minute, what about in between?

Here are things I'm fond of:

- **Accomplishments**
  - Numbers, percentages, dollars, awards (be certain not to include a former company's proprietary information)
- **Charts & Graphs are:**
  - Eye-catching
  - Can hold lots of information in a small space, and
  - All men try to figure them out!
- **Timelines**
  - Where you worked and when
- **Schools & Training**
  - Can be a separate page, or
  - Can be included in the timeline
- **Associations**
  - Shows depth of experience
- **Progressions**
  - Arrows pointing at an upward angle

    - When you did what and where
    - Can make reader see promotions
- **Consistency**
    - If you can show consistent increases, awards earned over time, or promotions, you can make the case for what you will do for the new company
- **Buzz terms**
    - What are the current crazes and hot topics in your industry?
- **Logos, flags & graphics**
    - A picture beats a thousand words
    - Let the reader read what s/he will into your "presentation"
    - Technically, borrowing someone's logo isn't legal, but only 1 client I know has received a Cease & Desist order
- **Few words!**
    - Lots of white space.
    - No "Death by PowerPoint!"
    - Shoot for no more than 10 pages
    - Invite a conversation

A few ideas to spur your imagination:

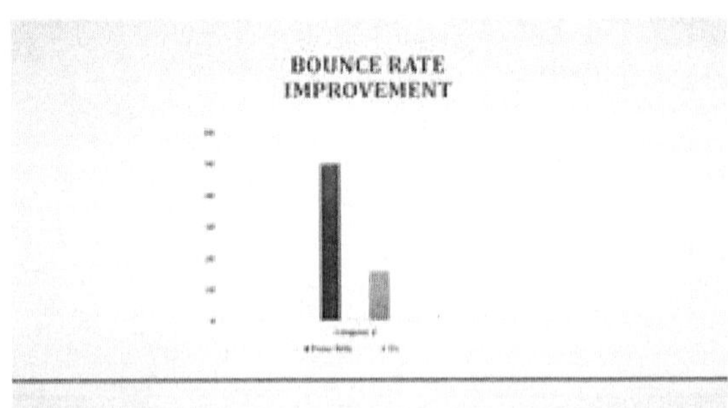

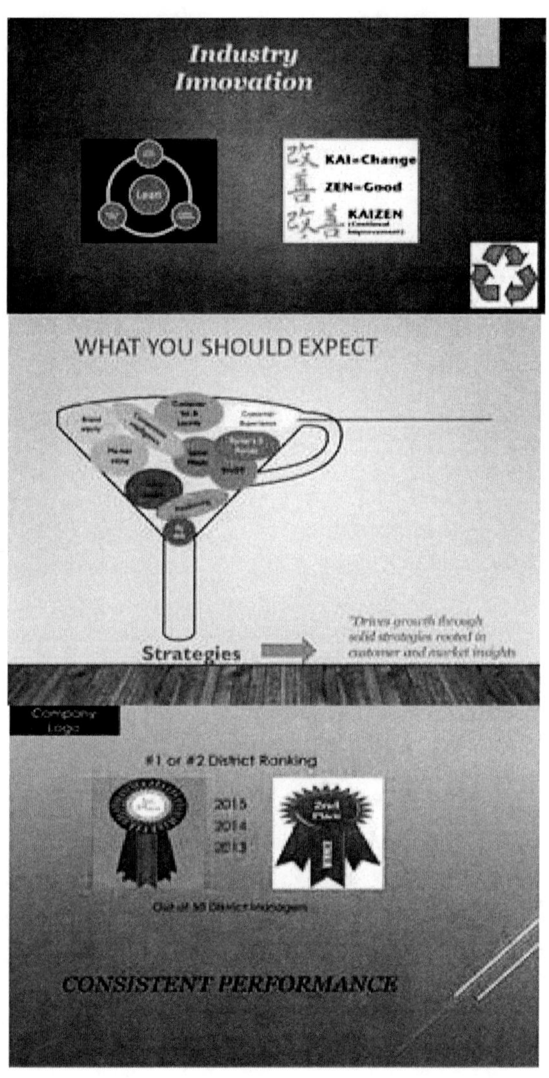
Industry
Innovation
Lean
KAI=Change
ZEN=Good
KAIZEN
WHAT YOU SHOULD EXPECT
Strategies
"Drives growth through
solid strategies rooted in
customer and market insights
Company
Logo
#1 or #2 District Ranking
2015
2014
2013
2nd
Place
CONSISTENT PERFORMANCE

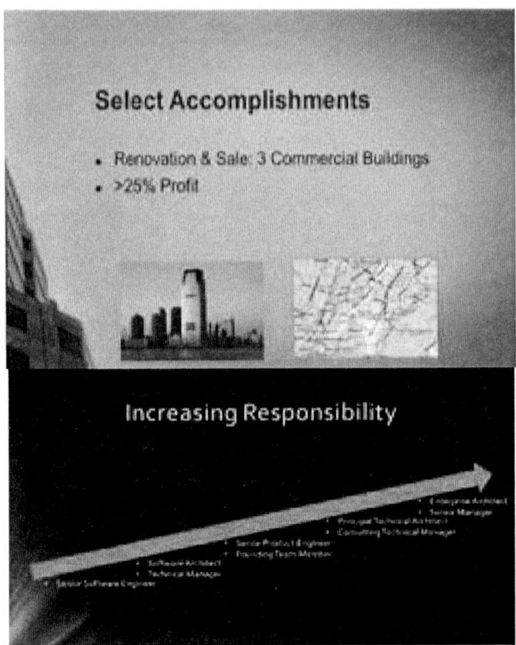

These are just a few of the examples of what can be done to tell your story in a few pages without boring people to death with paragraphs that won't be read. Sorry, I couldn't use examples with logos included because I'd like to keep my house. (Your use of logos should not be a problem because you're not trying to make a buck off them.)

What do I do with my Value Proposition?

You're on a roll with the good questions!1. Either upload your Value Proposition directly into two places on your LinkedIn profile – The Intro and Current employer sections – or use SlideShare (you get some analytics if you add this extra step).

2. Invite people to view it (call to action), especially when you contact company officials, targets, or Recruiters.

3. Put it on a QR Code and add the QR code to your business cards and email signature.

Does my Value Proposition have any other use?

Even better question. The answer is: Yes! You can adjust, print, and bind your Value Proposition deck to use as a presentation tool during interviews, especially in final interviews, by adding the target company's logo and even a 90-day plan. What's included in your 90-day Plan is based on answers to questions you have asked during previous face-to-face interviews. You will be using the employer's own words.

Print your Value Proposition deck and have it bound. There should be one for each person in the interview, but they should be left as leave-behinds. You don't want them flipping through material while you're trying to present it (you should "own" this space). So, give them out just prior to leaving.

Other Tools

Biteable: I like using multiple methods to reach people. Some people like words, some like images, and others prefer video. I want to appeal to the senses that turn people on and you should consider using different methods to reach employers, too.

My website designer, Don Harris, told me about an interesting tool. It's called Biteable.com, and I fell in love with it from the start. You're able to create short videos. I created brief videos explaining the services I provide, saved them to YouTube, then added them to my website (check it out), theHIREDguy.com. Here's a slide:

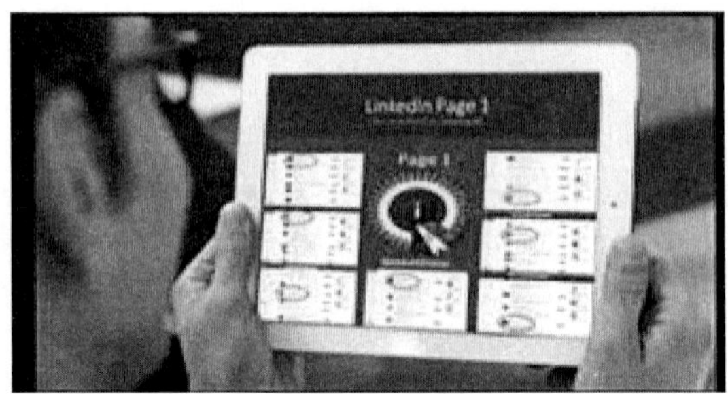

This one has someone who's "looking at his computer" reading about my LinkedIn Page 1 service. After a few seconds, he thumbs the screen to the next bit. What shows up on the screen is something I created. There are many templates to choose from, different animations, timing, and even background music.

You may want to consider Biteable to tell stories (and get people's attention) in a little different manner.

QR Codes

I'm not very tech savvy (honest), but if I were in job search mode, I would add a QR Code to my email signature and business cards, so I would appear more tech intelligent than I am.

What's a QR Code?

Here's an example I pulled from the internet (hope there isn't something bad in it):

QR Code stands for "Quick Response" and the technology was invented by Toyota for the automotive industry. They can hold volumes of information of all types, including images. There are a gazillion QR Code generators including, some business card printers like Vistaprint.

You can upload your resume (yuck), Marketing Brochure, Marketing Plan, Value Proposition, and/or video material. Most of all, they show (or intimate) that you are keeping up with the changing times.

There are also potential negatives, including that few people read them (through their smartphone) because they can carry viruses; but, if your intent is similar to mine, who cares?

Business Cards

Some candidates feel they don't need a business card. I know of no coach who would agree with that statement. A business card is another method for introducing yourself, sharing your brand, and networking.

The basics of business cards include your name, desired job title, phone number, email, and LinkedIn addresses. You may want to include some (not all) of the following:

- Graphics (branding used throughout campaign)
- QR Codes (see above)
- Picture (I'm not crazy about this)
- List of attributes

I recommend high-quality paper. Don't print them yourself (every time I've seen this, the end product was cheesy). If you use slick paper on the front, use a matte finish on the back. Remember, there are two sides to a business card. Don't waste this valuable real estate, but leave enough space on the back for the recipient to use for notes. Get 500 and give them out like candy at Halloween.

I must admit to some prejudices about relying heavily on business cards as a marketing tool:

- Alone, they don't separate you from the pack (if everyone has a business card, how does yours make you stand out?)
- They usually get thrown into a stack never to be seen again.
- There's no follow-up by either party.
- People either don't know what you're looking for or what it is you do.

A way to get around these challenges is with a Marketing Plan. It's like a second bite at the apple.

Marketing Plan

Question: What's the difference between you while in job search mode and a business?

Answer: Very Little.

Just as a business would develop a Marketing Plan, so should you, but for a different reason. Many Marketing Plans are created to give bankers a clear vision of the company's position to secure funds. Your Marketing Plan will be designed to give the contacts you make through networking a clear vision of what you do, what you bring to the table, and what direction you hope to take.

Virtually everyone in job search has business cards and an elevator pitch. Neither say much and both are forgotten within moments. A Marketing Plan is a great method for follow-up, clarification, and connection. Unlike a resume, which is a backward-looking document, a Marketing Plan focuses toward the future.

It gives greater detail of who you are, what you do, and the direction you hope to take with the goal of your contact being able to "see you" better. With luck, s/he will also think of companies or contacts they're aware of and will share with you. Ideally, this will help get the word out about you to fresh contacts.

A Marketing Plan should contain the following:

- **Contact Information** - Same as on your resume, the heading of your Marketing Plan must have your name, city and postal code, telephone number, and LinkedIn address. I believe you should also state your desired job title.
- **Positioning Statement** - This is similar to your Elevator Pitch, except it should focus on how you help companies as opposed to just titles you "had." Here's an idea:

  Continuous Process Improvement Manager

  Eliminating Inefficiencies
  Improving Quality
  Increasing Customer Satisfaction
  Growing Revenues
  Positively Impacting the Bottom Line

  Focus more on skills and competencies. Include things that differentiate you from all the other candidates. Also, if different from your current location, include target geographic areas.

- **Core Competencies** - Include 4-8 core skills or competencies you bring to the table. You can include a Value Proposition table here, as well.
- **Target or Type Companies/Industries** - Give an idea of what your direction is. Name areas of general interest (e.g. Consumer Products and specific companies you're interested in. (I love using company logos here; an idea I

first saw, loved, and stole ... errr ... borrowed from marketing genius Rick Steinbrenner.

- Don't focus only on mega-corps. Small-to-midsize enterprises (SMEs) account for 97% the total number of companies in America. They can be more nimble than big companies and they certainly relish people who can wear many hats.
- This document will probably go to contacts you meet at networking events, not directly to prospective employers. Your Marketing Brochure or Value Proposition deck is better used in those situations.

After you have mailed your Marketing Plan to your target contact, you need to follow up with a phone call. Schedule regular email updates to the database you will create as you add contacts. Let everyone know of your progress and other news. Ask what you can do for them and thank them for and ask them for continued assistance.

"In times of change,
learners inherit the earth;
while the learned find themselves
beautifully equipped to deal with
a world that no longer exists."
-Eric Hoffer

Chapter 8: Let's Roll

"Planning is bringing the future into the present so that you can do something about it now."
-Alan Lakein

Pre-launch & Launch Checklists

It's about time to get this show on the road, but first we should make certain everything is as close to perfect as possible. Here's a checklist you may want to take advantage of:

	Spelling
	Proofreading & Editing
	Voicemail
	Email Signature
	Online Reputation
	Contact Contacts
	Reaching Out
	Trial Balloons

Spelling Schmelling

Much has been written about common errors that bring down a job seeker's candidacy. One of the most frequent errors is mistakenly using the word manger (as opposed to manager).

Even I was surprised when I typed manger in the LinkedIn search bar: 541,533 people in my network have that word somewhere in their profile. Funny, right? It's even funnier to note that clicking on jobs versus people revealed 5,890 job postings misused the manger, as well. Of course, this isn't an excuse.

Nobody cares about spelling or grammar anymore! Look at Twitter and Facebook! Who has time to mess with that?

You do. You want to be better than the other candidates (and companies), right?

When I first met Kat Phillips, she was a technical editor and proofreader for states working on legal documents about a foot thick. She now works as a freelance editor and proofreader. She has ... ahem ... made me aware of a mistake or two over the years. I think you'll enjoy and appreciate her perspective and suggestions.

Even Your Tiniest Mistakes Can Count Against You

As a jobseeker, if you don't make the time, then you won't make the cut. In many cases, your resume/LinkedIn profile/website/introductory email is your first chance to make a great impression. Telling a Hiring Manager you're "detial-oriented" will get you dropped in the recycle bin immediately, because that manager will say, "What kind of work will you do for the company if that's the kind of lack of detail-oriented work you do for *yourself*?"

Yes, most word-processing software will point out minor mistakes you make, and even better, correct them for you! And if you trust that, allow me to direct you to damnyouautocorrect.com. Fun for texts, not so much for your professional image. Consider this: "I spent six months working with a dedicated broad, and we increased profits by 10%." Your software did that for you. You're welcome!

If you really think you don't have the time or talent to nitpick your way through your words, then pay a professional to do it. You can hire one from Fiverr or Upwork for less than 50 bucks. And before you snort and say, "Heck, I'm a good writer. It shouldn't cost 5," ask yourself how much your future career is worth.

Whatever you do, don't ask your mom or your best friend to do it, unless one of them is a professional proofreader. Average readers catch a few things but not everything, and you need to catch *everything*. You never know what error will catch a reader's eye, but errors always send up yellow flags. You want green all the way.

Proofreading & Editing

As much as catching misspelled words is important, catching grammatical errors is equally so. All your documents should be proofread and edited, multiple times and by someone other than you. See, we often read what was *intended* versus what is written, others often catch those errors. Additionally, I recommend people reading your material do so aloud and slowly. If it doesn't sound quite right, it won't be read well by your target audience. As Kat said above, you need to catch everything.

Voicemail

The old saying, "*You never get a second chance to make a first impression*," is especially important during job search. People who do not know you will be calling and leaving a message (sometimes), if you don't answer. What impression does your voice message leave someone with?

Having your children leaving a message or some inside joke might be cute, but it's not professional. You need to make a good impression, or at least not make a negative impression. Here are a couple standard voice messages:

1. Hi, this is <u>Name</u>, I'm currently unavailable, but if you leave your name, phone number, and message at the tone, I'll get back to as soon as possible. Thanks.
2. You have reached <u>Phone number with area code</u>, no one is available to take your call at this time, but if you'll leave your name, phone number, to whom you wish to speak, and a message at the tone, that person will get back to you as soon as possible.

Speaking of voicemail, consider signing-up for Google Voice (while you still can), especially my female readers. Although I have heard Google may discontinue Google Voice, as of the time of this writing, it's still available. I believe it's safer than strangers knowing your phone number.

You will be assigned a number by Google (some people have chosen numbers in the past). It will be your Job Search phone number. When a third-party calls, you will know it's job related. There's caller ID, so you will get a number and possibly the caller's name. By the way, it's free.

Online Reputation

It's a long-held truism that job offers are contingent on background and other checks, often including a drug screening. (In case you weren't aware, marijuana remains in your system for thirty days, so I recommend pot smokers get off the stuff and stay away from it while in job search. Even second-hand pot smoke can be picked-up in the tests).

The last time I had to take a drug test was when I was named Vice President of Sales and Marketing for a small pharmaceutical company in New Jersey. I'd been working for the better part of a week when I was told I needed to submit to a urinalysis. No problem, right? I jump in the car, find the office, fill out the paperwork, and excuse myself. I couldn't go to save my soul. Finally, it dawned on me that I was totally dehydrated. The only fluids I had consumed all week were a morning cup of coffee (a diuretic) and a cocktail with dinner!

That night I remedied the situation with adequate fluids. I returned to the doc-in-the-box and took care of the test. Before leaving, I asked the staff how old they were. I laughed and said I hadn't used pot in their lifetime.

So much for my "drug story." This section has to do with the potential perils of a bad online reputation.

Online Reputation? Quit acting like an old fart, Al!

My flatulence aside, let me share (again) the frightening information from a CareerBuilder article by Rosemary Haefner. Think about these numbers if you don't believe what you say and do online can affect your job search:[38]

- 48% of employers research candidates through Google and other search engines
- 44% research candidate's Facebook activity
- 27% check out your Tweets
- 23% review candidate's posts and comments
- Much of this research occurs PRIOR to a phone screen or interview!

What can I do about it?

First, you need to check yourself out ... on a regular basis. I recommend you search Google, Bing, Yahoo, and even YouTube every three months. Here's how:

1. Sign out of any email account associated with the platform to search (e.g., close Gmail if checking yourself on Google);

---

[38] Rosemary Haefner, Think Before You Post: Your Online Presence Can Cost You a Job, CareerBuilder, June 26, 2014.

2. Go to each platform individually;
3. Enter "your name" (in quotation marks);
4. Click Enter;
5. Check all iterations of your name (Jill Schmill, Jillian Schmill, Jillian A. Schmill, Jillian Ackerman Schmill)

Check what page you find yourself on. Don't forget to search for images of yourself. If you find undesirable content, seek to find the posting entity then ask the person to take it down. If it isn't taken down, your best options are:

- Add lots of content with your name included;
- Create a personal website (not my favorite idea);
- Write a personal blog post;
- Comment on many people's blogs;
- Set-up Google Alerts for professional industry material to write about and comment on;
- Whatever content you post, make certain it's keyword loaded;
- Add images to your posts and blogs where possible.

When you "Google" something, how many pages of results do you search. For the vast majority of us, the answer is only one page with few ever going past page three. Recruiters and professional search companies usually take the same tact. Your goal should be to push the offensive material to page four or further.

Email Signature

What's at the bottom of emails you send? Nothing, right?

What do you think will happen if you send me an email asking for an introduction to someone, but that target person can't easily respond to you?

Nothin!

Right.

An email signature is a simple, yet essential method to help others introduce you to potentially important individuals. It's also another method of continuing your brand identity. Make it easy for people to get hold of you by including a signature at the bottom of your emails and smartphone messages. It's simple. All email services and smartphones are similar. Here's how it works for Gmail:

- Click on the gear on the top right-hand side of your screen.
- Click settings.
- Scroll down the next page to where it reads Signature on the left-hand side of the page.
- Include the following (at least)
    - Name
    - Desired job title
    - Phone number(s)
    - Email
    - Address
    - LinkedIn address
    - Click Save Changes (you'll have to scroll down).

Make it easy for people to contact you! You will get contacted more often.

Note: Don't forget to do the same on your Smartphone!

Contact Contacts

Now that you are ready to launch your Marketing Campaign, I recommend an initial 2-pronged attack to all your friends and some foes (you'll understand in a minute). Let's start with your friends, your contacts. Let them know your employment situation. Don't be embarrassed! If they haven't gone through a period of transition, odds are they will. Let's set up an email like this:

> *Wanted to share an unfortunate update;*
> *Like so many others, my job up and disappeared. So, I'm in full job search mode.*
>
> *I'm seeking a job in (this, that or the other) industry and looking for a position with the title of_________ (specifics are important). I have already updated my LinkedIn profile and resume and I have some cool "marketing materials" I'd love to share.*
>
> *I'm not asking you for a job, per se, but if you become aware of something close or you can think of someone in the industries stated, I'd greatly appreciate an introduction. As they say, it's not what, but who you know.*
>
> *I'll keep you in the loop as things progress.*
>
> *Maybe you could find some time to share a cup of coffee. I'd love to catch up.*

Remember, this may be the "Social Media Era," but job search is still a contact sport. Schedule regular monthly follow-ups (less often and you're out of sight, out of mind. More often and you become a pest). When you have news, though, be sure to send all your contacts (even those who didn't respond) a positive update.

Use Excel, Google calendar, or any contact relationship management (CRM) device. Even a desk blotter works, although it's hard to carry around.

Here's another opportunity to utilize the Google Alerts you have established. When something of interest comes across your screen, share it with colleagues, your LinkedIn Group members and connections, and even former vendors. By taking these steps, you will be a resource (not a spammer) and you're less likely to be forgotten.

Practice, Practice, Practice

Remember in the previous section when I said to contact friends and foes? I'll make my case starting with a couple of clichés; the first is: "Amateur athletes practice until they get it right; professionals practice until they don't get it wrong." The second is: "Take the play in Poughkeepsie before bringing it to Broadway." (You can afford to fix mistakes in practice or in the boonies, it can be fatal on the big stage.)

You're going to make mistakes in the early stages of your Marketing Campaign. You don't want to make them with key individuals at target companies! Start your campaign with 5-7 companies you don't want to work for. Set the companies you WANT to work for aside for a week or two and focus on a few Dirt Bag companies.

As a sales manager, I always had my reports take this tact. Whenever we had a new product to launch or new marketing material to present, I instructed the sales reps to start with the clients who, if the reps screwed-up, it didn't much matter.

Doing this helped my region and its representatives win awards. It will help you, too.

Start by sending a Marketing Brochure to an Executive at one of the companies you don't want to work for. Send it by regular mail. Add a personal note saying you thought s/he might find it interesting and that you'd like to follow-up on a specific day. You actually will have to call and then ask for advice (never for a job) and also ask if the person has a moment (never a few minutes) to offer you advice.

Light this Candle!

The early stages of the American space effort were plagued with delays, destroyed rockets, and desperation on the part of scientists, officials, and astronauts. The first "Free Man in Space" was Alan Sheppard. A funny scene in the movie, *The Right Stuff,* was when Sheppard sat for hours in the space capsule on top of huge amounts of highly combustible material. Delay after delay followed other delays. In frustration, Sheppard called flight control saying, "Why don't you fix your little problem and Light this Candle!"

Let's light this candle and launch you into space. Here's a checklist to make sure all is ready:

	e-Resume (for electronic submissions)
	Job Boards (Resume uploaded to Indeed, etc.)
	Interview Resume
	Optimized LinkedIn profile uploaded
	LinkedIn "Share Profile Edits" turned back on
	LinkedIn Let Recruiters know you're open to new opportunities: On (Yes)
	Other Social Media (Profile uploaded as desired Google, Twitter, Facebook, and/or others)
	Marketing Brochures

	Business Cards
	Marketing Plan
	Google Alerts
	Networking Events

e-resume: Upload to the Job Board(s) of your choice. Use this version of your resume when applying to posted jobs. Remember to include a customized Cover Letter as the third page of each submission.

Job Boards: Indeed is a must, Ziprecruiter is growing, and whatever others you choose is up to you, but you will need to regularly update all these. BTW: Google has introduced its job search engine (about time).

Google Jobs aggregates positions and its algorithm searches for other valuable information. Business Insider's Aine Cain has a thorough article on it.[39]

Interview Resume: This should be printed on paper with high linen or cotton content. Gray, buff, or pale blue are recommended because they will stand out in a stack of other resumes. Your Interview Resume should be mailed or handed to human readers.

Optimized LinkedIn Profile: In today's job-search world, LinkedIn is most Recruiters' #1 search tool. Make certain you are found when they search for your desired job title. Have someone NOT connected to you check to make certain. A friend or spouse temporarily dropping you as a first level connection works the same as a Recruiter's search. Also, "make it hard to find you," so it's easier for Recruiters to find you.

---

[39] Ann Cain, Google launched its own job search engine — here's how it works, *Business Insider*, June 22, 2017.

Other Social Media Sites: Choose the ones best for your age, profession, and visibility. Remember, whatever you post one place should be consistently placed on all platforms.
Marketing Brochures: After sending out and following up with the "Dirtbag" companies, schedule to mail no more than five Marketing Brochures to target companies. Never send them to Human Resources because they wouldn't know what to do with them. I like mailing them on a Wednesday or Thursday, so you can follow up the following Tuesday. Never call on Monday (Mondays are "Meeting Day). If, after 3-4 attempts at contacting the target Executive have failed, cross them off your list.
Business Cards: Make certain your business cards are perfect as soon as you get them. Make changes if necessary. Five Hundred will hopefully see you through this process.
Marketing Plan: Proofread thoroughly. Like your Marketing Brochures, a Marketing Plan can evolve over time. Print only a few at a time.

King of the Hill

As a kid, we played something we called, King of the Hill, where we would battle our friends to stay on top.

In job search, your goal is to stay on top in views of your posted resume (Job Boards) and LinkedIn. The more often you're viewed, the better your chances of getting a call. Your strategy is to get more views more often. Here are the tactics to accomplish those goals.

LinkedIn: you should be posting industry-related content daily. Review your Google Alerts for topics of interest. Reposting is the easiest thing to do, but if you want more impact, take the material from multiple sources to create your own, personally created content. Do NOT use other people's content without giving attribution. Name the source (author), publication, and date. Use Bitly.com to create a shortened link from the long URL.

LinkedIn used to give members a running total of profile views, including a chart. It was the most important set of statistics LinkedIn provided. As of January 2017, that service ceased to exist. As of publication, the best it offers are the ones below:

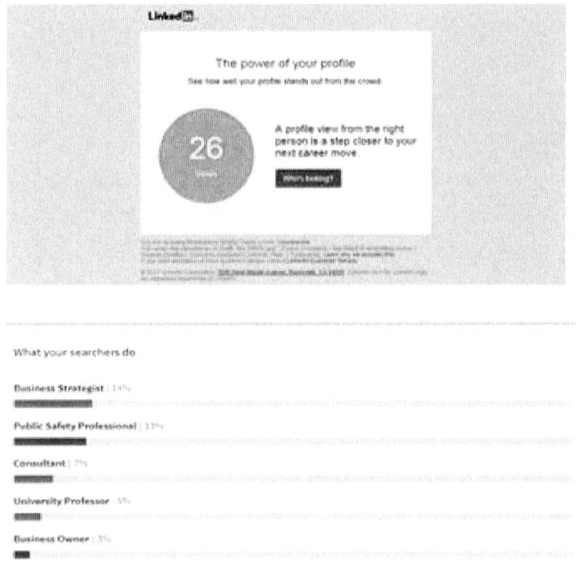

Check this information every week (more about this later). At the same time, attend to your posted resume on the Job Boards of your choice.

"You can't discover new oceans
unless you have the courage
to lose sight of shore"
- Andre Gide

Time to set sail!

Chapter 9: Plan Your Work; Work your Plan

"When you know what you want,
you realize that all there is left
then is time management.
You'll manage your time to achieve
your goals because you clearly know
what you're trying to achieve in your life."
-Patch Adams

Focus to the Finish

If I had my druthers, you would wake up at the same time you did when you had a normal job, go immediately to where you keep your computer, and start your job search day. You would start before you showered, fixed a cup of coffee, ate, or got dressed. You would turn on the computer and begin by applying to the job(s) that came to you through the search agents you set on job boards.

Next, you would read through your google Alerts, post some of the more interesting ones to your LinkedIn activity board and groups, and then create original content for others. By this time, you're hungry, thirsty, need to go to the bathroom, or smell so bad you can't stand yourself. You would then turn off your computer, take care of the normal things of life and focus on the real ways of finding a new job.

There are those who say I live in a fantasy world, but a guy can dream, right?

In the previous chapter, you were given pre-launch and launch checklists. Now I'll share methods for maximizing the efficiency of your Marketing Campaign.

Playing Password

It makes a lot of sense (and is safer) to have different passwords for every entity requiring one, but remembering them can be a nightmare. A couple solutions include using Microsoft Notepad or Excel. You can maintain your passwords by entering each entity by name alphabetically.

Another method for more complex passwords is LastPass.com. There are both free and paid versions, but even the pay version costs next to nothing per year (about a buck per month as of publication). They offer multiple methods of encryption. One is by setting up an account that stores your passwords on the cloud, another is kept on your device only (the company doesn't even have access to it) and another offers two-factor authentication. (Thanks to my friend Charlie Brown for making me aware of this; he says, "Always protect yourself with two-factor authentication.")

Filing & Finding

The phone rings. It's a Recruiter!

The Recruiter's asking if this is a good time to talk. You make the mistake of saying yes (see interview chapter for why you should avoid impromptu interviews).

How do you find the information you put together for that company? Do you fumble through a stack of sent resumes? How about thumbing through a bunch of manila folders?

Yikes! You're flustered from the beginning (and end!).

Using hanging and manila folders is fine but they need to be labeled and organized for the different aspects of your Marketing Campaign (alphabetically by industries for example). You also want to save all live prospects on a cloud server (Google Drive is one of many) as opposed to just in your computer's hard drive or on a thumb drive. If on the cloud, no matter where you are you have access to your files.

> I had the bright idea to move my former (HIRED!) clients' files onto a thumb drive. As things happen, my main work computer had a problem. After it was fixed, a former client became a current client again (no offense, but I'd prefer it if I never saw former clients or YOU again ... and I mean that in the best possible way!). Re-opening the file wouldn't a problem, right? It's on my handy-dandy thumb drive. Oh, no. The thumb drive was corrupted, and my Mr. Fix-it computer guy's best option was to send it to Washington DC where, for a cool grand ($1,000), they *might* be able to recover its contents. I lost all those files. Don't be like me!

Set up Folders and subfolders (as you did with your files) in a Word Document or the Apple equivalent. Keep active prospects together and remove those companies who have made the mistake of passing on you. You want to find files in a hurry. (And save them on the Cloud!).

Old Fart Email

One of my recurring workshops concerns search strategies for Baby Boomers and older Gen-Xers. I ask all workshop participants to fill out a sign-in sheet. I ask for their name, phone number, and email address. The next day, I send one email to the lot of them, so they can connect on LinkedIn (you can't have too large a network while in job search).

Every week I warn the participants about being regarded as an old fart by Hiring Managers. One way to be pigeon-holed as not keeping up with the times is to have an antiquated email address. My favorite Old Fart emails are MindSpring, Bellsouth, AOL, and a handful of others.

> I must admit to maintaining an AOL account. It's the same one I used for years. I keep it because I've tried to get former co-workers and reports to use my Gmail address, but they never seem to get the hang of it. I keep and occasionally check my AOL account because I don't want to lose contact with those old friends, but it's not my primary email address!

Do yourself a big fat favor and get a Gmail, iCloud, .me, or other, up-to-date email address. Though I really do not like Gmail (if you make the mistake of deleting a thanks email out of a long string, the entire string is gone, and you play hell finding it. You can also forward a string of emails to someone in error).

> My favorite story is about a client whose area of expertise is cloud sales, SaaS. When he sent me his old resume, it had a Bellsouth.net email address! I yelled (by email), "Get an iCloud account. It's part of your Personal Brand!" He apologized by saying he had an iCloud account, but hadn't changed his resume.

Pick a Card, Any Card

Always carry business cards with you. When at a networking event, association meetings, and other target-rich environments, put received cards in a different pocket than where you keep your business cards. Using a business card case is even better. Follow-up the next day with the people you met. Send a Marketing Plan or Marketing Brochure and a personalized LinkedIn connection request. Remember to offer to help THEM and ask to meet.

Marketing Plan

These can be sent either by mail or electronically. When following up with people you met at networking events, sending them electronically is better because of speed, although sending them through the mail gives you a "second bite at the apple."

Google Alerts

Scan the headlines of each alert on a daily basis. Search for material to add to your LinkedIn groups, the "Share an article, photo or update" section on your LinkedIn Home Page (hopefully, they will rename this section), and select connections. Use this material to write LinkedIn Articles, blog posts, and to start "conversations" in your LinkedIn Groups.

Networking Events

Search for business-to-business events, association meetings, and conventions in your area. You want to surround yourself with people who are employed. They tend to know where jobs are and where/when openings might be coming. Many companies pay referral fees, so it's often in your contact's financial interest to help you. Don't forget to reconnect with all of your contacts. You never know who knows whom.

Views = Victory

As a kid, we played something we called, King of the Hill, where we would battle our friends to stay on top (not many hills in New Orleans. Levees, yes; hills, no). In job search, your goal is to stay on "top of the hill" in views of your posted resume (Job Boards) and LinkedIn profile. The more often you're viewed, the better chance of you getting a call. Your strategy is to get more views more often. Here are the tactics to accomplish those goals.

Job Boards, you'll need to schedule, and update, your posted resume every week (I recommend doing this every Friday before noon). Don't scream! Some Job Boards allow you to make minor changes such as: This Friday go to the Job Board, find your posted resume, change a comma to a semicolon then hit save. Bingo! You're king of the hill! Next Friday before noon, change the semicolon back to a comma. Boom! You're king of the hill again (many Recruiters look for "newly uploaded resumes). Unfortunately, you may be forced to take your resume off the site then upload it again. The process only takes a few minutes and isn't it worth it to get more Recruiter views? Besides, what else are you doing Friday morning?

Speaking of Job Boards, only apply to a handful of job postings per week, as Richard Morgan suggested earlier in the book. You don't have time to follow-up if you apply to many more than that. Besides, the higher you are on the professional totem pole the less likely you are to find a job through online applications and job boards.

Deb Dib stated in a jobhunt blog, "Job boards don't work well, especially at executive levels, but most executives think they do. They also think executive Recruiters will get them a job, even though most statistics say far fewer than 20% of senior-level jobs are landed through Recruiters and job boards, combined."[40]

In a further example, PBS' Nick Corcodilos addressed a former CEO who had applied to more than 1,000 posted positions over a four-year period, resulting in a whopping four interviews and zero offers. Corcodilos offers, "The best source of information for [executive] job hunters is indeed in articles in the trade magazines and business press, both in print and online. Those articles don't discuss jobs, but they tell so much about the work that they are great tipoffs to career opportunities. These articles are also where you meet the people who make industries go - engineers writing about their companies' technologies, marketers debating the value of product strategies, executives discussing the viability of businesses, reporters revealing the stories "'between the lines"' that might affect an entire

[40] Deb Dib, 10 New Executive Realities, JobHunt blog.

industry, and much more. These are the people who can lead a job hunter to a company, if the job hunter will only take the initiative to get in touch with them."[41]

Find a company's pain point(s), then show how you can solve the problem (without giving away the store) and a position can be created for you. Be aware, this process takes time.

LinkedIn: You should be posting industry-related content daily. Review your Google Alerts for topics of interest. Reposting is the easiest thing to do; but, if you want more impact, take the material from multiple sources to create your own, personally created content. Do NOT use other people's content without giving attribution. Name the source (author), publication and date.

Use Bitly.com to create shortened links from the long URLs.

Job Boards (again)

You've already figured out I'm not much of a fan of Job Boards, but some people still get jobs this way (generally speaking, the younger and more junior level you are, the better your chance of getting a job through a job board). Besides, it is widely stated that only 15%-18% of all jobs are posted on job boards (there's great debate here). All age groups of Americans spend an inordinate amount of time online and on job boards according to Millennial Branding.[42] (Yes, you have seen this before).

Topic	Type	Boomers	Gen-X	Millennials
Percent of Time Spent Searching and where	Online Offline	96% 4%	95% 5%	92% 5%
Primary Search Tool	Job Boards	87%	82%	77%

---

[41] Nick Corcodilos, Ask the Headhunter: Why Can't the Former CEO Get a Job? PBS Newshour, Jul. 1, 2014.

[42] Dan Schwabel, The Multi-Generational Job Search Study 2012, Millennial Branding, September 24, 2012.

To increase your effectiveness further than suggested earlier, consider the following:

1. Search Agents
    a. Create search agents sending the jobs meeting your criteria into your inbox
    b. Narrow your focus if you start getting too many jobs that aren't quite right
    c. Broaden your search criteria or search for a different title if you're getting too few.
2. Time: Limit the amount of time you spend applying to posted jobs. I wasn't joking in the introduction to this chapter! A couple of hours is the maximum you should spend on job boards.
3. Research and Reach Out:
   After applying to a posted job (on job boards, LinkedIn, or elsewhere), research people who work for the company. Look on LinkedIn (see where having all those connections can help?).
    a. Look for people who might be the Hiring Manager, posting agent, or other insider
    b. Send LinkedIn Connection requests
    c. Send your resume and Marketing Brochure (NOT you're Marketing Plan), but not at the same time.
    d. Don't waste time! When companies have "enough" applicants, they stop looking even though the posting may remain.

Human Resources

I should make a couple things clear. Most of us throw around the terms HR and Recruiter as if they mean the same thing; they don't. Human Resource departments contain two major components: Benefits and Talent Acquisition. TAMs are the ones who do the hiring as opposed to dealing with things like insurance. Both groups work for the company itself. Sometimes TAMs are Recruiters, but not usually.

Recruiters, on the other hand, can be divided into two groups, retained or contingency.

A retained Recruiter is engaged by a company to find talent and receives part of its fee upfront (a retainer) whether they deliver the employee or not. In today's world, retained Recruiters are almost exclusively hired to find executives. In many cases, these folks "steal" executives from other companies (often specific companies). So, even the best executives are unlikely to make any headway with a retained executive Recruiter.

Contingency Recruiters get paid a commission several months after the candidate is hired. Let's spend a little time on this type Recruiter since they're the ones searching to fill jobs. Remember though:

None of these people work for you!

From this point forward, we will be discussing TAMs. These are elite professionals.

Most of us are instinctively territorial, we want to guard what is ours. This has never been truer than with companies' Human Resources department. For some, formally applying is a requirement. So, apply already! (then do whatever you can to get directly to the Hiring Manager).

It's been my experience, working with TAMs at career ministries, that TAMs are caring individuals who want to help people find employment. The problem is they're doing the work that 2-3 people used to do (bet that sounds familiar to many of you, as well). They don't have time to address the needs of every person who applies for a job. As a result, they increasingly rely on Applicant Tracking System software and Artificial Intelligence to find candidates (these also save companies money).

You will often find the name of the TAM (Posting Agent) in a job posting. This is especially true on LinkedIn. If so, you should send a note directly to that person, aside from your electronic submission of a combined resume and one-page cover letter (a three-page document). That combination itself might help you avoid the Black Hole.

Your note should be no more than a few lines and to the point. It should include the job title and requisition number (or job ID#, if either is available). State that you have already applied, you meet or exceed the requirements (don't bother them if you do not meet most of the requirements), and that you're requesting that he or she flag your application. It doesn't always work, but what does? Besides, it can't hurt to try!

Continue to research and use your connections just as you would in any other instance, but you will at least have covered all the bases by having applied as the company required.

Some final things about TAMs that you should be aware of come from a *Fast Company* article by Amy Elisa Jackson, *"This is what Recruiters are thinking when job seekers are unsuccessful."*

1. **We could have gone higher if you had negotiated** – They almost never lead off with the best offer. There's almost always room to negotiate a better salary and benefits. We will discuss further in the Interviewing chapter.
2. **You never had a chance after making that bad first impression –** The old adage stands, "You never have a second chance at making a good first impression."
3. **Your references were not very flattering** – Ask permission from people you want to use as a reference and for goodness sake, make certain anyone you're using as a reference will give you a good one.
4. **I back-channeled you and found the truth** – With the advent of LinkedIn, TAMs can find people they know or are connected to who can get the poop on you.

5. **We already gave the job to an** in-house employee – Although totally unfair to the outside candidates, it's perfectly legal to run a dog-and-pony show of candidates so everyone can claim they conducted an exhaustive search. Asking about Internal candidates will be covered in the Interview chapter.
6. **Your last few Social Media posts were deal-breakers** – Everything you put out there is searchable. Please re-read the section in the previous chapter concerning Online Reputation.
7. **The team is dragging its feet waiting for another candidate's response** – Yes, the delay could be that they wanted and offered the position to someone else and you are the fallback position candidate.[43]

Recruiters

Earlier, we divided Recruiters into two groups: Retained and contingency. Again, they do not work for you, they are both acting on behalf of the employer.

A Recruiter attempts to find talent to fill a job requisition. They cannot create a job for you. Most employers (the company with the need) farm their requisitions out to multiple Recruiters or recruiting companies, which put agencies in competition with each other. They gather "paper" on several candidates, pre-screen them, then present the best ones to the company. They don't really care which one gets placed as long as it's their candidate.

Recruiting has never been easy and is much more difficult today. Some still take the time to specialize in a small number of industries and have built solid relationships with both clients and candidates. Unfortunately, these people are few and far

---

[43] Amy Eliza Jackson, This is What Recruiters Are Thinking When Job Seekers Are Unsuccessful, *Fast Company*, Sept. 11, 2017.

between. These Recruiters maintain a database of qualified candidates.

Most Recruiters these days are "peckers" (pecking on a keyboard all day). They rely almost entirely on electronic methods of search (Boolean searches and Job Boards). Unlike the professional Recruiters described above, some of these folks are required to place ads on Job Boards just to troll for resumes to "sell" prospective employers to use them. There often is no job associated with their job posting!

It's fairly easy to recognize the difference between the two groups. The latter group that is likely to resemble Barbie and Ken dolls and conversation with them is about that vapid.

It's the former type Recruiter you should seek. Once you've established a relationship with your Recruiters, try helping them. They work on commission, right? Ask what job titles they're seeking (never ask for the companies) explaining if you know someone good, you'd like to pass them to the Recruiter. Try to find 2-4 Recruiters to work and stay in touch with (no more than that).

Miles Jennings, former Recruiter and current CEO of Recruiter.com, lists five key things to consider when you go shopping for one:[44]

1. Past Success,
2. Company Knowledge,
3. Project Information,
4. Technical Understanding,
5. Personal Connections

Keep a couple of things in mind:

---

[44] Miles Jennings, 5 Signs of a Great Recruiter, *Recruiter*, Mar. 11, 2013.

- A Recruiter can't help you if s/he doesn't have a requisition for your job title;
- Don't expect many phone calls. They're too busy;
- Recruiters work on straight commission;
- Never them ask for the name of the company;
- If using a Recruiter, don't also apply online.

Reminder: "Headhunters" exist only in deepest, darkest Africa and in the movies. If a Recruiter doesn't have a job requisition where you fit, s/he won't give you the time of day.

I highly respect good Recruiters, finding them is the challenge.

The World's Rarest Animal

Have you ever seen a purple squirrel? No, seriously, have you? I didn't think so, but they must exist based on some of the requirements in job descriptions.

Actually, a Purple Squirrel is the term used by Recruiters asked to uncover candidates with superpowers, who can leap tall buildings in a single bound, whose teeth sparkle when they smile, have 20 years' experience in everything imaginable, and are willing to go to work for peanuts. Check that, peanut. Singular!

No one can meet the requirements of the Purple Squirrel candidate. No sacrilege intended, but the Lord Jesus Christ wouldn't qualify for some jobs today!

The *Daily Kos* reported, "the interview process at many major companies has just about doubled [time] in three years."[45]

---

[45] by Gravlax, Purple Squirrels and Unemployment, *Daily Kos*, May 6, 2013.

Hiring the wrong person is expensive. Consider the manpower cost during the search period; lost productivity of taking the Hiring Manager away from his/her normal duties; expense of lost productivity from the ,open position itself; and the inevitable post-hire learning curve. The greatest potential cost, however, is that many companies are more likely to fire a scapegoat who made the "wrong" decision.

The increase in required skills is understandable to a certain extent. TAMs don't want to make too many mistakes. Not even do they want to go through today's hiring process. They are likely to "lack the requirements" (including the violet hue).

Most of us target posted jobs where companies are seeking to fill a position with our job title (you most likely don't need this book to tell you how to do that!). Now, imagine working for a company you WANT to work for and enjoying your work day - what a novel idea!

Career Coaches

As I've said before, I have great respect for good Career Counselors and Job Coaches (and great disdain for bad ones). I freely recommend other coaches in my weekly workshops and want to surround myself with the most talented ones.

A close friend knew someone in the Denver area who was seeking a Career Coach in his locale. He asked if I knew someone. I didn't, so I turned to my trusty right arm, LinkedIn, to search for Denver-based coaches. I must have read through 10-15 profiles before I discovered Lisa Carman. Everything she talked about in her profile was spot-on with today's job search world, so I recommended Lisa to my friend's friend.

I connected with Lisa on LinkedIn and reached-out to her by email. I wanted to let her know she might be contacted. I also wanted to let her know I agreed with her stated methodologies. We have since chatted. I asked her to share her perspective on why hiring a Career Coach can be a smart investment in your future. Here's Lisa Carman:

> **W**hy should you hire a career professional to support your professional employment efforts? Simply put, because you matter, and your career is important. Writing an effective resume can be a truly difficult task and having a strategic approach to job transition can mean the difference between employment and unemployment, career growth and career stagnation. Investing in your career growth is one of the best investments you can make.
>
> If you have considered hiring a career transition professional such as a Resume Writer, Career Coach, or LinkedIn Profile Writer, it is probably because you have experienced the difficulty, frustration, and mystery of the job search first-hand.
>
> A job search is not what it used to be. Gone are the days of the Sunday paper "Help Wanted Ads," mailing out a few resumes, and sitting back, waiting for the offers to roll in. Today, you are confronted with online job boards, increased competition, and an in-depth applicant screening processes.
>
> The job application process alone has evolved quickly, in large part due to the sheer volume of people constantly changing companies and roles. Faced with hundreds of applicants for any given opportunity, businesses need automation to deal with the influx of applications. This automation facilitated Applicant Tracking Systems (ATS), which screen out "unqualified" candidates based on word matching and algorithms and reduce the resume pile to manageable levels.

Due to ATS screenings, you no longer have "a resume." Instead, you have multiple versions of a master resume document. Your resume lets you target positions of interest and function as a fluid marketing tool. To satisfy ATS and HR screenings the resume must meet specific criteria, namely matching the keywords found in the Job Description. Your resume must transform into an adaptive framework customized with keywords, skills and experience that are relevant to each role you pursue while honestly portraying your value.

Re-inventing yourself to pursue a career in a new direction can be an even more challenging exercise. Whether considering new opportunities in your current company or an external career transition, the key is to gain a sense of focus and create an action plan that will prepare you for the next leap upward, sideways, or out.

A career coach can facilitate this decision-making process by using assessment instruments, providing an objective perspective, and offering industry expertise and knowledge. One of the main functions of a career coach involves built-in accountability and client support. For many facing or seeking transition, this outside help is the missing puzzle piece to the career picture.

Should I bother with LinkedIn? Isn't it just my resume again? LinkedIn is a professional networking tool that allows you, passively or aggressively, to present your skills, thoughts, experiences, and interests to other professionals and companies in an online forum. If your LinkedIn profile is not up to date, you risk being perceived as disinterested in opportunities, unwilling to adopt new technology, or uncomfortable with professional social media.

> LinkedIn is the current tool of choice for companies and Recruiters when it comes to finding talent.
>
> Building a relevant, compelling profile and maintaining an active presence on LinkedIn promotes your expertise and interests and enables you to assertively spread that information to a larger audience. A LinkedIn expert will know how to craft your LinkedIn Profile AND teach you how to market your brand so that you start getting "found" by Hiring Managers and Recruiters.
>
> Still pondering about hiring a career coach? The real question is, "Why wouldn't you?"

As Lisa said, hiring a Career Counselor or Coach is a smart investment. Compare the cost of being out of a job for even a few extra months versus the fee for hiring a professional Career Counselor. I see it as an investment versus an expense, even at a time when your normal reaction is NOT to spend money.

Contacts

You were asked in Chapter 2 to compile a list of 200 or more contacts. As your search progresses, that number will grow. Unfortunately, keeping track of them all can become a daunting challenge. Organization is essential.

If you're like me, you have multiple email addresses and, of course, sets of contacts in each of them. I recommend consolidation in two places:

1. In your primary email account (Gmail)
2. A Contact Relationship Manager (CRM)

I suggest doing this in two places just in case something weird happens. You don't have to buy an expensive piece of software to accomplish these goals. Creating an Excel spreadsheet works fine. Of course, you'll need to update these files because you will be adding contacts regularly (you should) and occasionally delete the uncooperative people from the list.

You need to schedule sending updates to your personal connections every 6 weeks to 2 months. I recommend using either Google Calendar or an Excel spreadsheet. You will want to update them on your search, share a joke, or something else they might find interesting. Keep things upbeat and fresh.

Set up a similar time frame with the contacts you meet at networking events and uncover in your research. For these, you will want to:

- Send a Marketing Brochure,
- Invite them to coffee,
- Share industry information (Google Alerts).
- Don't forget:
- Pick up the phone!
- Ask what you can do for them!

Targeting (redux)

What percent of companies have or need someone who does what you do? Do you know all those companies? Let's try targeting unknown companies.

There are multiple ways to uncover companies. Two of the best are Zoominfo and Hoovers. To use these resources best, consider using the computers at your local public library instead of your home computer. Why? Because those companies want to charge you for accessing the information and you have already paid the fee, at least part of it. You paid for it in your tax bill.

Go to their website and type in a company name. Part way down the page there should be a list of other companies. Some will be competitors, others might be similar, suppliers or ancillary organizations. Suddenly, you have a list of 20 or more target companies!

While you're at the library, you may want to explore ReferenceUSA. It wouldn't surprise me if your local library had access to this site. Of course, doing a Google search for companies in desirable industries is a method easily conducted from your home.

The first company I worked for was Kimberly-Clark Corporation. They're the manufacturers of Kleenex facial tissue among many other things. I Googled "facial tissue" then clicked on images. A boatload of brands appeared. I clicked on a brand I'd never heard of, Aryuv. The company name, XinTeng, and its website appeared. I clicked on the web link and found that it's a Chinese company supplying paper products for several companies in the states including a "Green" company. Bingo, a potential target.

I've tried several times to do the same thing on LinkedIn with only moderate success. I just don't find its search algorithm very friendly, but with all the changes being made by Microsoft, I'd keep trying.

You questioned my sanity when I suggested you build a list of 200 or more target companies, remember? Think of this: Manta.com shows there are about 165,000 companies in the Atlanta metro area, 200 companies would be 1/12th of 1% of that total! (Maybe I'm not quite as crazy as you once believed).

Okay, you've found some companies, now you need to find people at those companies to target. Here's where I like to use LinkedIn (if you have unlimited search through one of the premium packages, take advantage of the deals LinkedIn offers). By the way, as of this publication, a way to avoid the "Professional Search Limit" is to use a mobile device! Other ways to find employees and executives include Glassdoor and Data.com (formerly Jigsaw).

LinkedIn is increasing its importance as a site for job postings. Some years ago, I was asked to create a workshop specifically designed for the challenges faced by millennials and younger Gen-Xers. What I uncovered can be used by people of all ages.

When searching for jobs, you may see who the posting agent is. This is a target! Go ahead and apply, then research the posting agent. When I did this for the young worker workshop, I uncovered the posting agent's work phone number, email address, and Twitter handle. Although I would never Tweet, you should pick up the phone. Call; leave a short, prepared message that you applied to **JOB TITLE** with **REQUISITION NUMBER** (if one is listed) and why you want the TAM to pull your resume from the queue.

You may be the only one to reach out and I bet your resume will at least be read by a human being. Your chances of getting an interview improved dramatically.

Resources available to you include:

- Your contacts
- Google
- LinkedIn
- Data.com
- GlassDoor
- Manta
- YouTube
- Twitter
- Your Library for:
    - Hoover's
    - ZoomInfo.com
    - ReferenceUSA

Networking

Sources claim that anywhere between 40% to 80% of all jobs are found through networking (not surprisingly, networking events hold dear the highest numbers). I can't put my finger on any concrete statistics regarding the effectiveness of networking as the *only* element of a job search, but I can attest to the fact that the clients who combine all sorts of networking with LinkedIn page-1 positioning, a properly formatted resume, various marketing documents, and extensive interview training tend to get jobs much more quickly. In short, networking is an integral part of a successful job search plan. [46]

An outstanding networker is Tyrone Griffin. The first time I encountered Tyrone, I was in the audience listening to a speech on time management during job search. Tyrone said, "If it's 3:00 PM and you have your Bunny Slippers on, you're NOT looking for a job." What a mental image, but he's 100% right! (Check out Tyrone's podcast, Bunny Slippers are Evil). Tyrone is a master networker, as well. I don't think he's ever met a stranger and I'm glad to call him friend. He offers his insight:

> **N**etworking and impression are exceptionally important. There is no reason to ever leave a bad impression. Even if things do not go the way you hope, be gracious in defeat as well as victory. Not everyone you meet will be able to recommend you for a position (most will not), but you never know who will. Good impressions are remembered, bad impressions are never forgotten.
>
> True story, I was "between opportunities" as we say because it sounds better than "unemployed." Out of the blue, I got a call from a Recruiter I had not spoken to in 5 years. He had an opportunity on his desk, he'd remembered me from all those years ago, and wanted to know if I was currently looking. We talked that Monday morning, and by Monday night I had an interview scheduled for Wednesday. By Friday I had an offer in hand. First, yes, the Lord works in mysterious ways. Second, this

---

[46] Monika Morrow, Networking, Not Internet Cruising, Still Lands Most Jobs for those in Career Transition, *Right Management*, May 8, 2013.

> Recruiter kept my number because I'd made a positive impression on him 5 years earlier. Like I said, good impressions are remembered.
>
> I've seen people in job search burn bridges because they never expect to be in job search again. You never know what tomorrow will bring or whose path you will cross again. I currently work alongside someone who was my boss at a different company. Always be aware of the impression you give. You cannot afford to let your guard down at the wrong time. The person you think isn't important enough to be professional toward today may be the hiring manager looking across a table at you tomorrow. To that end, job search is a process, not a goal. There is no "I've perfected job search and can now find any job any time." The best generic advice I can give someone in transition is to be flexible, nimble, and able to adapt. The "great idea" that worked yesterday may blow up in your face tomorrow. Just like marketing, you test, learn and retest.

I'm in favor of all manner of networking, even more so today than in years past and for candidates of all ages (especially younger people because your age group is perceived as lacking social skills). Still, I can't endorse going to multiple events attended mostly by unemployed people. Please restrict attending such events to those where there are workshops or speakers whose topics are of interest or address your areas of weakness.

Besides your current, traditional contacts (family, close friends, acquaintances, clients, vendors, former bosses, and colleagues, etc.) there are several other traditional methods of networking including:

1. Career Events (Church-based and secular)
2. Speaker events
3. Accountability Groups

I've already shared my two cents' worth on spending a lot of time where most people don't have jobs. My biggest fear is you being surrounded by negativity. The same applies to accountability groups where there isn't someone keeping the tone positive. If a keynote speaker has a topic of interest, go! This is especially true if it's a motivational speaker.

Attending networking events are wonderful in theory, but can be an exercise in futility if you go to them without a plan of action. Job networking expert, Jay Litton suggests the "3-to-1 Rule." Your weekly goal would be to attend at least one networking meeting per week and to get three meetings or introductions per networking event. The follow-up is for the contact to give you a "warm introduction." Your goal for the next meeting is to uncover two (or more) others in the target company to contact. You want to get as high up the food chain (company executives and people in your area of expertise) as possible and build a bank of insiders within the target company.

In addition to the familiar methods of networking, you should explore some of the many non-traditional methods of uncovering potential helpful contacts. Those methods include both personal and electronic networking such as:

1. **Business-to-Business Events:** Recognizable to most of us are Chamber of Commerce events. I think there is a Chamber chapter in every city, municipality, and burb. The Chamber is an organization of business owners (you know, people who employ others). Often, someone can attend one (1) Chamber meeting if with a member. After that there are fees involved. There are certainly many other B2B events near your area. Some have fees involved; others do not (do your research in advance). These meetings are also potentially rich environments for candidates who are prepared.

Don't be a wallflower, socialize. Step out of your comfort zone. No one there will bite. They are there for many of the reasons you are there. Besides, B2B events are superior to venues without employed people!

Networking Strategies include:

- Spend a little time with a lot of groups,
- Move from group to group,
- Ask questions,
- Listen intently,
- Offer your help, if you can,
- Introduce yourself, and give elevator pitch,
- Don't ask for a job!
- Offer your business card to everyone,
- Ask for their business card and
- Follow-up within 24 hours!

2. **Conventions**: Don't think of conventions as just those huge gatherings in enormous centers. There are those, and if you can get to the venue, you have the potential for meeting some of the heavies of target companies. **Note:** Executives are almost only in attendance during the first couple days of major conventions. Gaining access to the convention floor can be tricky, unless you can talk someone you know out of their badge, but don't be discouraged. You can run into many in middle and upper management in the halls outside the floor itself and in the dining areas (great place to "run into" targets). Even better is to send invitations a couple weeks in advance to "cultivate" target executives. (I did this once for a poorly attended convention and got meetings with six executives, including five company presidents and a Director).

Remember when setting up meetings to ask for a moment and that you're seeking advice. In the meetings, ask about how you can improve your Marketing Brochure or Value Proposition deck. Have a resume ready in the event they ask for one, but don't ambush them with a resume (immediate turn off!). Ask if there is anything you can do for them and keep in mind they may not have a position for you today, but may have one in the future - *they* change jobs too!

As always, exchange business cards, follow-up and contact them with pertinent industry or personal (positive news about them) information. You want to stay on their radar. Being persistent is an attribute, being a pest is not.

In addition to the mega conventions, there are many regional ones. Check these out, but know that few executives attend.

3. **Associations**: The last time I looked, there were ninety-seven associations listed on Weddles.com. weddles.com/associations

Most industries have local or state associations. These are a great way to meet industry insiders.

Many attendees, officials, and speakers are open to a brief meeting. Don't overplay your hand. This isn't the time or place to overtly ask for a job. Once again, you're asking for advice, sharing your Marketing Brochure, Marketing Plan or Value Proposition deck. It's not the place for a resume, but have some just in case. And, as always, ask how you can help them!

While there are fees involved with these events, you may try volunteering with a promise to join once you land a job. Remember to bend over backwards for anyone who gives you a helping hand.

4. **LinkedIn:** As stated repeatedly, LinkedIn is a great tool for uncovering people at target companies. There is a lot of hit and miss, but with over ½ billion members as of 2017, talk about your target-rich environments!

5. **Meetup**: Many towns have business-related meetups. Check them out on the web.

One last thing, if there are cocktails served at the events you attend, I recommend not imbibing; but, if you do, limit yourself to one. As Tyrone said earlier, bad impressions are never forgotten.

Job Fairs

Step right up folks. See the five-legged goat and the bearded lady. World's only $2.00 freak show!

My goal for this book is to present every method for job search, including ones I don't care for. Job fairs are firmly implanted in that category. I'm not the Lone Ranger with my belief. Eve Tahmincioglu of the blog CareerDiva.net and Careers on NBCNews.com describes job fairs as, "A lesson in futility."[47] If two opinions aren't enough, Ask the Manager's Alison Green writes, "[Companies] are wasting the time of the employees they send, and they're wasting the time of job fair attendees like you."[48]

I've glanced at the employers participating at many job fairs during the last decade and have been generally unimpressed. There have been many companies seeking to fill entry-level, hospitality, and labor positions. Companies specializing in landscaping, call centers, pest control, security, and insurance (Quack, quack), are also common participants, yawn! Your job title, not so much.

---

[47] Eve Tahmincioglu, Do Job Fairs Really Help You Land a Job?, Careers on CNBC, Apr. 27, 2009.

[48] Alison Green, Have you Ever Gotten a Job from a Job Fair?, Ask a Manager blog, Mar. 14, 2011.

There was a huge job fair at the largest convention center in my city a of couple years ago. It was set in the middle of the summer with big-name companies participating. People came out in droves, dressed to the nines. Candidates were lined up outside in the sun by the hundreds. Seeing the images on the evening news reminded me of the opening line from Harper Lee's, *To Kill a Mockingbird,* "[they were] like soft teacakes with frostings of sweat and sweet talcum" (spoken in my breathy, saccharine southern drawl).

Resumes were "accepted," but many of the attendees who finally got in were told to "apply on the company website." Most got nothing more than sweat-soaked clothing and a wasted day. On the other side of the coin, job fairs on college campuses can be of be some benefit to graduates and focused job fairs can be productive. If there are workshops or tutorials for attendees, by all means take advantage of them, but don't expect much more.

If you're going to attend a job fair, you should prepare for it fully:

- Pre-register - some companies review resumes seeking top talent for openings;
- Research employers - Will any of your target companies be in attendance?
- Bring multiple resumes, Marketing Brochures and Value Proposition decks (attach to resume; they will make you stand out);
- Prepare for typical interview questions and have your practiced elevator pitch ready to roll off your tongue;
- Follow-up: Ask the best method with which to follow-up. If the reply is a *don't call us, we'll call you* sort of thing, search for people outside HR (do that anyway);
- Network, network, network!

It's commonplace for companies trolling for "bodies" to attend these events. If your life's ambition is selling googahs at a mall kiosk, a job fair may be just the ticket, but if you have higher aspirations, consider spending your time elsewhere.

Volunteering During Job Search

A great way to clear your head, step away from the computer screen, set aside the never-ending application process, and possibly have some fun is through volunteering. It could also lead to your next job.

Much to my wife's chagrin, I set aside 20% of the normal work week for volunteering (mainly job search tactics workshops). It led me to career counselling and writing my books (neither of which are positive financially, but they are highly rewarding in other ways). It's also something I recommend all candidates do during job search, as well as after you are hired.

Many companies will choose a person who volunteers over equally qualified candidates who do not. It speaks to your character, "Wow! Even when s/he was looking for a job s/he gave back" or "This is a well-rounded, well-grounded person who thinks of others" or "This is a team player." Unfortunately, many who volunteer forget to make potential employers aware of it.

You could offer your time as a laborer at a homeless shelter or a soup kitchen, but consider some of the more practical advantages of your time when seeking a position to volunteer for, such as:

1. **Staying up-to-date** – Many employers feel you lose your skills immediately upon losing your job. (I'm not sure how that happens; did you take some skills-depleting kryptonite?) Volunteer doing something that hones your skills or keeps them up-to-date.
2. **Filling the Gaps** – Gaps in your resume are Red Flags to employers. Some will ask, "What have you been doing since you left your last job?" Explaining that

you've been volunteering is a way to assuage their fear of a gap.

3. **Meeting Potential Employers** – Lots of business owners and executives volunteer. Those who do are often attracted to people who give of themselves, too. If they don't have a job for you, they may recommend you to someone who might. When rubbing elbows with others, people get to know your character and isn't that better than just an interview?

Volunteering can't help me get hired!

Think not? What if I told you that, "active volunteers were 27% more likely to get a job than non-volunteers." Those were the findings of a group of 70,535 people being tracked over a ten-year period for any relationship between volunteering and employment. They found that volunteering had a direct relationship with getting a job. Gender, race, age, ethnicity, geographic location or what the unemployment rate was at the time mattered [not] one iota.[49]

Anyone can find themselves needing a helping hand and you may find, as I have, that the person being helped most is you.

"We make a living by what we get,
but we make a life by what we give."
-Sir Winston Churchill

[49] Corporation for National Service, Volunteering as a Pathway to Employment.

Chapter 10: Interviewing

"Give me a lever long enough and
a fulcrum on which to place it,
and I shall move the world."
-Archimedes

Note: This is by far the longest chapter in the book and for good reason. Everything before this chapter was to get you in front of the Hiring Authority. Now that you're there, I want you to be able to differentiate yourself from the other candidates, so you can get HIRED!

Interview Did You Knows

Many of us are terrified at the thought of interviewing. You go in feeling certain you'll make a fool of yourself ("There's no chance of getting the job."); on the other side of the coin, some claim, "If I could only get an interview, I'd get the job." Both extremes are probably untrue. I doubt anyone died in an interview, and none of us are as good as we think we are. In any case, interviewing can be stressful. Confidence is crucial, and confidence comes from practice.

The great football coach, Vince Lombardi, said, "Practice does not make perfect. Only perfect practice makes perfect." Although I can't guarantee interview perfection, if you work on what's in this chapter, I promise increased interview success.

Were you aware that for some job requisitions, companies receive hundreds to over a thousand applications? One Fortune 150 Company was seeking a new administrative assistant. It received more than 1,200 applications! Those numbers have been the rule, not the exception, especially during economic downturns.

Pretend you were among that throng and you got a call. You would have been one of maybe 25 people out of the 1,200 to get a telephone interview. Shouldn't THAT instill some level of confidence in you? You qualify! They may not feel you're the perfect fit, but out of all those people, you were among the initial ones chosen.

If you get a face-to-face interview, you would be one of ten, maybe a dozen, chosen among the original 1,200. And, if you get to the final interview, you're competing against only two to three others. Every one of these steps is a reason to be confident and celebrate.

One of the people I'm most in awe of is Cindee Sapoznik, CLC. Cindee clearly has a passion for helping those who seek a hand up as opposed to a hand-out. For as long as I've known her, Cindee has focused her attention on teaching at-risk kids, women who have survived human trafficking, and those who are attempting to turn their lives around from substance and/or physical and other abuse. (The Atlanta area's 2myPlace and City of Refuge, for example)

Cindee has the ability to communicate with people who are, for good reason, skeptical and wary of others. She tells it like it is and these folks know it. One of Cindee's areas of expertise is interview training. She shares her thoughts with us in, *The Interview Process: What you need to know that "they" want to know.*

The Interview Process

It's all about self-confidence and clear direction.

Before you get into the meat of an interview, know that decisions are made by your handshake, ability to look someone in the eye (eye-contact), and clear pronunciation of their name (and yours).

You know the tall buildings with windows floor to ceiling?

Know that when you drive up for your meeting, you are being watched (not to make you paranoid, just aware!). People watch what time you arrive (you have an appointment time, remember) and how you are dressed. Are you glued to the phone, chewing gum, rushed, putting on makeup, or making last-minute hair adjustments? Any of these can be interpreted as having a lack of preparation, disorganization, or irresponsibility. You don't want to be known for any of those things before you walk in for your interview.

I always like to begin the interview "process" with a character-building workshop. You can't sell yourself to someone else, if you don't know who you are. So, figure out who you are (your brand), and what you will bring to the table for the position. Choose five words that best describe your qualities and work ethic. Then relate these attributes to how you work and what you are capable of accomplishing for them.

A question often asked is, "What do you feel is your greatest weakness?" Some companies, because of their human resource department, aren't even allowed to ask this! So, turn it around, "I don't really consider it a weakness, but rather an undiscovered challenge or skill that I'm working on." Examples include: lack of a second language or fear of speaking in front of groups. "They" want to see effort on your part, so your response would be, "Seeing the advantage of being multi-lingual, I'm taking Spanish lessons. I bought Rosetta Stone tapes, and I practice by listening to Spanish radio and TV channels," or, "I've joined a Toastmasters group to help me feel more comfortable in front of people and improve my presentation skills." (See how positive that sounds)?

Last, and most importantly, YOU MUST ASK FOR THE JOB!!!! This could look like, "Within the first 90 days of you hiring me, what are three of the most critical changes you want me to accomplish?"

Informational Interviews

Earlier we talked about the goal of networking: the 3:1 Rule. Meetings with these people can be called informational interviews and should be treated the same way you would any job interview.

As should be obvious from the name, your goal is to get inside information about the company, its "pain points," personalities, upcoming vacancies, executives and management in your area of expertise. In short, you hope to find ways to showcase your value to the target company and uncover champions to your cause.

Warm introductions have a higher percentage of success towards getting to the informational interview stage, but mailing an initial Marketing Brochure to target company insiders, especially executives, shouldn't be overlooked. I'm not talking an email (can you say delete?), I mean mailing a brochure with a note then following up with a phone call. If your material is impressive enough and you have uncovered a bright executive, there is a distinct possibility of, not only an informational interview with the executive, but the executive may issue a directive for your potential superior to meet with you.

Buying or Selling?

Interviews are buying and selling exercises. You are trying to sell your brand to someone who will be buying a product from someone; they will eventually make a hire (you or someone else). Think about your experience shopping for a car, clothes, or most anything. You may want to buy something, but do you like being sold? I didn't think so. It's the same with interviewing. You should present your selling points and allow them to make the purchase.

> When I was a young salesman, I was pretty good, but I was only out for me. I had a quota to make; I wanted people to buy my products and I wanted to make bonus money. Ay, yi, yi, yi,yi!
>
> At one point, my boss gave me the book, *From the Buyer's Side* (it's out of print). The book itself wasn't that good, but its title was excellent. When I looked at things more from the buyer's side than mine, my career took off because I would tell my clients if someone else's products or deals were better than mine. I was no longer seen as just another schlepper out to make a buck at everyone else's expense, I became a trusted resource and an honest broker. You should look at interviews in a similar fashion.

Let's look at interviewing *from the buyer's side*.

Hiring Manager Stress

Hiring can be as stressful for the Hiring Manager as it is for you. Did you know a Hiring Manager can be fired for making bad hires? Yet, most companies invest little to nothing to train managers in how to make proper hiring decisions. Considering the cost to a company whenever there is an open position, you'd think someone would invest the time and money to train Hiring Managers how to hire.

Think about the costs associated in having and filling an open position:

- Lost productivity (of the open position);
- Posting cost of a job requisition;
- Time cost of contacting prospective candidates;
- Multiple face-to-face interviews (incl. Panels);
- Lost productivity of the Hiring Manager being away from his/her normal, everyday duties;
- Training the new hire; and Ramp-up time.

None of these compare to the cost of hiring the wrong individual. As a matter of fact, an Australian survey of small-to-medium-sized enterprises found employers were dissatisfied by nine out of ten new hires within a year of hire.[50] Talk about costly!

Want to know a secret? Hiring managers dislike the hiring process as much as you.

Why?

Because they're paid to do a job and the hiring process gets in the way of them performing the duties for which they're being judged. Take a deep breath, you're about to help your next Hiring Manager, and get a job in the process.

There are many interview styles and I'll try to share as many of them as possible. Although the styles may vary, the desired outcome is the same: the best person for the opening gets hired. But the fit must be mutual; the street runs two ways. If it doesn't fit for you, it won't be a fit for them either.

Think of job search as looking for a spouse. First, you must like each other. You go on a few dates of sorts, better known as multiple interviews. What's the best way to get to know someone on a deep level? Questions and answers from BOTH

---

[50] Stephanie Zillman, Ninety Percent of Employers regret recent Hires, *Dynamic Business*, Mar. 4, 2014.

you and your prospective employer. In her Forbes article, Liz Ryan penned a list of ten objectives of every [good] Hiring Manager.[51] You would be wise to work on lines that address these desires. Hiring Managers seek:

1. Someone who can think on their feet.
2. Someone who looks beyond the work on their desk to spot potential problems and head them off before they get bad.
3. Somebody who jumps in to help when there's a problem.
4. Folks with fantastic follow-through.
5. Someone who has great ideas and is happy to share them.
6. Somebody willing to learn, and to teach what they know.
7. Someone who has a sense of humor.
8. Dependable candidates who keeps their commitments.
9. Somebody who can work with a wide variety of people.
10. Candidates who see a job as more than a way to get paid.

Q4U

Questions, Questions, Questions ... A long time ago, a former boss told the story about an article he read claiming trial lawyers are such good listeners, they can break into a sweat while listening to testimony. At the same meeting, he mentioned salespeople were among the worst listeners. From that moment forward, I swore I would improve my own listening skills and work on those skills with my employees.

If this is about listening,
why are you talking about questions?

As you know, I've spent my career at every level of sales, from "carrying a bag" to the executive suite, and as my former boss said, salespeople are terrible listeners - for the most part. They're so intent on presenting the features and benefits of their product(s), they never bother listening to the customer or

[51] Liz Ryan, Ten Things Every Hiring Manager Is Looking For, *Forbes,* Jan 9, 2018

seeking to understand the customer's needs. I dubbed this "the show-up and throw-up" method of sales (it's as ugly as it sounds). Things clients are saying tend to be manipulated into answers. In my 30+ years as a Hiring Manager, candidates tend to do the same.

A question I always asked sales job candidates was, "What's the most important trait all outstanding salespeople have in common" Most say they're good talkers. You should have seen their eyes become saucers as I shook my head. After a tense moment, I'd say, "They are all phenomenal listeners. God gave us one mouth and two ears for a good reason. They should be used in that proportion."

I like the saying, "When you talk, you are out of control. When you ask a question, and listen to the answer, you're in control." This is as true in interviews as it is in sales or life itself. (I get into a lot less trouble when I let my spouse talk than when I try to interject!).

You need to be asking as many questions as you answer during interviews. I mean LOTS of questions. Ask questions from the beginning to the end. But you should ask the right type question for the situation. So, let's discuss the different type questions and what information you might expect from each type.

There are two general types of question: Open-ended and Closed. In sales training classes, they are known as Open Probes and Closed Probes.

A closed probe elicits one of three one-word answers:

- Yes
- No
- Maybe

A single word answer is all you're likely to get since there is little else for the respondent to add. This type question is usually used to confirm information.

A variation of a closed probe would be a choice question such as, "Do you want me to start tomorrow or would you prefer Monday?"

Other examples of Closed Probes include:

- Will my next interview be at the home office?
- Is it true, that the company's best year ever was last year?

Open Probes (open-ended questions) are designed to get the interviewer to "open-up" and provide expanded responses with information s/he never intended to share. You want to ask these type questions as often as possible. The more you know about the job, company, Hiring Manager, pain points, etc., the better positioned you are to touch on the things the Hiring Manager wants from a new hire (you).

Typically, open probes contain one of the following words:

- Who
- What
- When
- Where
- Why
- How

Examples of open probes include:

- **Who** will I be reporting to?
- **What** will you want me to focus on in the first 30, 60, 90 days after you hire me?
- **Where** (with whom) will my next interview take place?
- **When** do you plan on making a hiring decision for this position?

- My research tells me our products are superior in almost all categories. **Why** would a client go with someone else?
- **How** did you achieve your position?

Can you see how these types of questions can be valuable tools to gather information and make the interviewer feel even better about you as the candidate of choice?
Going back to lawyers for a moment, they ask lots of both type questions and practically salivate when someone freely answers open-ended questions. But they only ask questions they think they know the answers to or are seeking additional/unknown information for.

It's largely the same for you in your interviews.

What is it you know (or don't know) about the target company, industry, the competition, market position, company's struggles and successes, opportunities, and so on?

You need to work (well in advance) on a series of open-ended questions to ask during interviews. Be sure to research the people you'll be interviewing with, especially your Hiring Manager. Remember, all questions should flow in a conversational manner, so practice asking them in Mock Interviews with someone you respect and trust.

Keep in mind, though, there are unknowns that all the research in the world won't uncover. So, some of your questions must be asked to position yourself (your product) in its most favorable light. Ask questions that might lead to an opening to present your Value Proposition, what you bring to the table, and how you satisfy the needs of the Hiring Manager and company. Such as:

- What traits do your best employees have in common?
- Was the person I'll be replacing promoted (fired, retired, etc.)

- How long has the position been open?
- On what should I focus to be your best employee on your staff?
- How quickly do you want to fill it?
- Was the person I'll be replacing effective?

Don't you agree that asking questions like these would provide better, clearer, fuller information than you might otherwise uncover? Could the information you uncover with this type question be used later in the interview (or subsequent interviews)? Can your answers to THEIR questions give them a clearer of you? Are they hearing the substance they seek from their candidate of choice (you)?

Note: Resist the temptation to break a silence after you've asked a question. Let them think it through. Wait for as long as necessary for the interviewer to answer.

Sales Rule #1:
Ask a Question then...
SHUT UP!!!

Why?

> My first "real job" was with Kimberly-Clark Corp., which hired me when I was still in high school, believe it or not! One day I was working with my boss. I wanted to change the facial tissue section of a store to better showcase my Kleenex brands. I made my presentation to the store manager. He was thinking and thinking and thinking about it. I got antsy and started to blurt out another reason why my idea was a good move, but before I could get a phrase out of my mouth, my boss wrapped his island-sized paw (stole that line from a Jimmy Buffett song) around my

arm. I shut up in mid-phrase. The manager approved my suggestion.

When we were alone again, Pat said, never talk first. Let them think about it in silence, for as long as it takes. "Whoever talks first, loses."

Phone Interviews

The main reason I don't like most interview coaches (and books) is they focus on face-to-face interviews and forget that to get to the F2F, you must pass phase one: the phone screening interview. A phone interview is the initial conversation between you and your prospective employer. If the screener doesn't move you forward, you're toast.

Educating you to perform better on Phone Interviews is important to me because, at one point, I was terrible at phone interviews! Let me explain.

We communicate more through body language than by words and tone of voice combined. (Communication: 55% Body Language, 38% Tone of Voice, 7% Words).[52] I love the study of body language. I'm a physically expressive individual. I "speak" with my body, hands, face, and especially with my tone of voice. (My daughter used to ask, Dad, why do you have your Mad Face on?" I was usually concentrating on something). This cost me jobs in the past.

The last time I was in job transition, I would get calls from companies I was perfectly qualified for, go through the phone screening process, and concluded I've done a great job. I would hear nothing (sound familiar?). This happened time and again. Finally, I realized I would be

---

[52] Unnamed Simply Hired Staff Writer, The Power of Body Language in a Job Interview, Simply Hired Blog, November 21, 2013.

nodding my head in agreement instead of verbally expressing myself. There would be these long pregnant pauses of silence with me nodding. What a dope! I don't want this to happen to you.

If you agree, say so. If you want to write something down, tell the person something like, "That's an excellent point, I hope you don't mind, but I want to write that down." No periods of stone silence, please.

You should prepare in advance for questions likely to be asked in your phone interviews. You have already prepared your S.T.A.R., R.A.T.S., and Red Flag stories. Next, you should check the internet for the currently "hot" (usually dumb) interview questions. Don't limit your research to just Google, YouTube is an excellent source of material.

I recommend creating a cheat sheet with single words in a column that remind you of anticipated questions. In an adjacent column, have single words that remind you of the answers to those anticipated questions. In a third column, list words that spark your memory for the questions you want to ask.

Listing the anticipated questions alphabetically makes for quick reference. Doing the same for questions you want to ask can be done similarly, but remember to add questions tailored to specific companies before scheduled phone interviews. Also, having a few of these sheets on hand can save your bacon if you make the mistake of taking an impromptu phone interview (more about that in a bit). This can be the outline of a "script." But, as with all scripts, "rehearsing your lines," will improve the play.

Phone scripts must be practiced but never read during the interview. You'll want to be able to ad lib, which is why your script should be no more than bullet points to remind you what you want to present and get you back on track if you go on a tangent or get lost.

NOTE: Use a large font size when assembling your script. Normal font sizes may be too difficult to read in an already nerve-bending interview.

One Ringy Dingy

Your first contact with your prospective employer will probably be with the person on the lowest rung on the HR totem pole. This person may not even work directly for the company itself, and the screener probably isn't even located in the company's office because much of this work is outsourced. Many of these people (throughout Human Resources) know little to nothing about the company, the industry, and even less about the job they're interviewing for. Don't blame them though. They're probably only given a script on a computer screen with questions popping up based on the answers you give.

So, the phone rings. You pick it up. Someone on the other end says, "This is lhfkmnbahas from, #$!@~(&)%)%$%^ Corporation, is this a good time?"

First, you probably had a fake heart attack from getting a call in the first place. You didn't catch their name, you don't know which company the call is from, and you're certainly not prepared. So, what do you do? You jump headlong into to the interview, right?

Bad move!

What you should do is ask the person to repeat their name and company, since you didn't catch it the first time they said it, and you want to write both down. Now's when you need to "massage the truth" a little. Tell the person you're expecting another call (you're expecting a call from another company sometime, right? But you just don't know which one yet) and ask if they can reschedule.

This accomplishes many positive things:

- **Preparation**: You can prepare yourself for the interview
- **Research**: You can research the company and maybe even the interviewer
- **Questions**: Prepare targeted questions to your script (based on your research)
- **Rehearsal**: Gives you an opportunity to rehearse your answers for anticipated questions and answers in your script
- **Demand**: Gives the interviewer the impression that you're in demand
- **Relax:** Through preparation you can relax and should have more confidence

Before disconnecting with the Recruiter, ask if s/he can send you a current copy of the job description. If you're getting a call for a Hidden Job, you don't have the job description. This is also a subtle way to get the email address of the screener, which allows you to send a note of thanks after the interview.

These tactics have the potential for setting you head and shoulders above the competition.

What if they say they can't reschedule?

I suppose it could happen, but in my view, any company that inflexible is a company you don't want to work for.

Two Ringy Dingy

The phone rings at the appointed time. Because interviews can seem confrontational (they want to ask all the questions and you feel like you're behind the 8-ball), I recommend diffusing all tension from the beginning. Show some empathy while trying to make a personal connection with the interviewer. You may want to try some of these ideas:

- Thank the person for rescheduling
- Ask if it's true what you heard about Recruiters doing the work of 2-3 people these days
- Ask how their week is progressing
- Ask where they're calling from and how the weather is
- If there is a common thread, say something about it (cities, schools, weather, etc.)

You should try moving your interview in any direction that can put you in a positive light. Asking questions from the beginning can do this.

You've made nice for a couple moments by asking some personal questions, now it's time to try to uncover information to help move you forward. I like starting with, "Do you mind if I ask a question before we get started?" (I've never known a Recruiter to say no). Follow up with, "Hopefully, you've had a chance to review my resume, what is it about my background that prompted you to speak with me?" (This question is even more effective when you have face-to-face interviews.) There are only three answers to that question:

1. The interviewer rattles off a handful of attributes you bring to the table. Quickly write them down. When finished, you thank the Recruiter for recognizing those traits, "When I read the job description, it practically screamed, *this was written for me!"* Plant the seeds that you're the right choice from the get-go.
2. You could be told that you had passed the initial screening and your name was assigned for a phone screening, meaning the person has no clue why you're being interviewed. Here's where you can say, "You were probably assigned to speak with me because I bring this, that, and the next thing to the table." (These will be keywords taken directly from the job description.)

3. Me being me, I have to throw a joke in here, so the third possible answer might go something like the Recruiter saying, "I have three thousand four hundred sixty-seven questions to ask in 3.5 minutes, but if we have any time left over, you can ask any question you want."

Let the Recruiter ask the question then answer it fully.

It would be great if you could interject another question or two to move from "confrontation" to conversation. Resist the urge to press. Unfortunately, many phone interviews are fully scripted, precluding much back and forth. At the end, however, you will probably be asked if you have any questions. Assumptive close questions can work.

Your goal for this and every other interview is to be passed onto the next phase. Assumptive close questions include:

- Where will my next interview be conducted?
- Who will I be interviewing with next?
- It's safe to assume you will be passing me to the next phase, right?
- What's the next step?
- Is there anything special I can prepare for my next interview?
- Will my next interview be by phone, video, panel, or face-to-face?
- Do you know anything about the next person I'm interviewing with you can share?

Enthusiasm sells. You must sound excited about the job. No one wants to hire Eeyore! (from Winnie-the-Pooh).

One way to ensure excitement is to stand during your phone interviews. Have your notes and cheat sheet laid out on your desk for quick reference and note taking. Remember to tell them you're taking a note (don't be like I was!).

End the call with appreciation for the interviewer. You may even ask if there is a way to send a thank you note or email. Just asking this question is a positive in your favor. It's an additional "selling point" for you. *"It was great getting the chance to chat with you today. I hope the opportunity presents itself for us to meet face-to-face after I start with the company!"* In your note or email, be sure to include the job title, requisition number (Job ID#), and the job's location (city and state).

Dollars & Scents

Everyone seems to dread the salary question. What a stinkburger! You're likely to have been asked on the applications you've already submitted, and you'll certainly be asked in your phone screen interviews. There are two quite different questions you'll be asked:

1. What were you making?
2. What do you want to be make?

The answer to the first question is pretty much straightforward. (**Note:** Some states, starting with California, are no longer allowing salary history questions, thank goodness). You can add benefits such as bonuses, car, and maybe a few others, but there's not much wiggle room. It was what it was. There are a few notable exceptions:

- If you made a lot more than you will be making with your next job, you need to make them aware you know and accept the reduction (I had to do quite a bit of explaining when changing from my own company to a new, salaried position)
- You might have taken a "bridge job" outside what you normally would do professionally, in which case you explain, "That job allowed me to meet my family and financial obligations. I wasn't going to go on assistance."
- Or you can explain, "In my last position similar to this one..."

What you want to earn is a trickier question to handle. It's a parsing question. If you want too much (or too little) you can screen yourself out of a job. If possible, put on some music and do a little tap dance. Here are some possibilities:

- Can we get back to the salary issue a bit later?
- I'm sure you have a range for the position. Would you mind sharing it with me?
- I'm sure if we both feel this will be a fit, your compensation package will be commensurate with my experience.

Unfortunately, many phone screens require you to pony-up a number. Okay, so tell them. If it's too high, they'll let you know in short order. But they have a range, so should you. You should have three salary numbers:

- **Walk-away:** Can't work for that or below. If you have this number in your head in advance, you won't hesitate to tell them no thank you.
- **Pie-in-the-Sky:** This is what you would like to make in your wildest dreams. (I was once offered $40,000 more than my P.I.T.S. number once. It was the shortest tenured job I ever had. I knew they had a bad reputation and I took the job anyway. Big mistake.)
- **Goldilocks:** This "number" should be a range. It should be a realistic number, but don't be bashful! You're worth it, right?

Payscale.com is probably the best tool currently available to research salary ranges. Glassdoor has decent numbers (a bit on the low side). I've found salary.com to be difficult to use and LinkedIn's ranges, at present, are absurd. My suggestion is to have a range on the high side of the bell curve. Then ask again what their range is.

Still, do your best to avoid talking salary early on if possible.

Spontaneous Combustion

You've prepared answers to your potential Red Flags, STAR stories, and anticipated interview questions. You should also have some introductory or bridge statements to ease into those answers. I call the phrases, "Planned Spontaneity."

The traditional method is to pause prior to answering or repeat the question. Both are good. The former leads one to believe you're thinking of a proper answer. The latter confirms what the interviewer is seeking (it also buys you a bit of time).

On the other hand, you may want to take that slight pause then start with:

- I'm glad you asked that question ...
- Although not exactly the same, something like that happened to me ...
- We were challenged once ...
- We had a challenge when I was at XYZ Corp ...

Bridging statements can make your stories sound more spontaneous and natural. Try not to force your stories, but include as many as possible in a conversational tone. They will be taken in a more positive light.

Lights, Camera, Action!

As technology has improved, Skype, Zoom, and other video resources have become increasingly popular with companies. Remote interviewing is very inexpensive and highly inefficient.

Think about a company with a national or global reach. If either expanding or replacing someone, video can reduce or eliminate the cost of travel and its related productivity losses. This is certainly true for the initial contacts with large numbers of candidates.

Don't be afraid of a video interview. Think of it as a face-to-face interview with a camera and microphone. I prefer a video interview to a phone interview. For one, a computer's microphone and speakers are superior to most phones (especially VoIP). Difficulty hearing? Adjust the volume or use a headset. There isn't the echo, delay, or reverberation typically experienced with cell phones either. Best of all, you have the ability to read the interviewer's facial expressions and a little bit of their body language.

Some companies will have you go to their local office or to a rental office suite (such as Regus). Others will have you take the interview using your home office computer. If at a location other than your home, be certain to arrive early and ask for assistance getting acquainted with how the equipment works. You'll want to test out the picture-in-picture feature, so you'll know how you will appear to the interviewer.

Behave for a video interview in the same manner you would for an in-person interview. Dress properly, it matters! (This includes video interviews from your home.) I know of people who have dressed from the waist up, but one had to reach for something, forgot he was in his skivvies and they showed. He only realized what happened because the interviewer started laughing.

There are a few "musts" regarding video interviews:

- **Camera and microphone**: Almost all laptop computers have these built in. Desktops do not. External mic/camera combinations can be purchased for less than $100 at any office supply store.
- **Placement:** If using a laptop, set the computer on a stack of books so you can look directly into the camera's eye, otherwise the interviewer will be looking up your nose! Make sure you are centered in the screen.
- **Clutter:** Remove all clutter from view. At one point, I had a thoroughbred racing picture (my horse won!) in view while another time I had vitamin and prescription bottles in plain view (not smart, Al).

- **Silence:** Take a video interview when and where you have no noise. You don't want screaming children, lawn mowers, or barking dogs around.
- **Shuffling papers:** Try not to shuffle papers because the microphone will pick-up the sound.
- **Food & Drink:** I shouldn't have to include this, but never eat during a video interview and limit any beverage consumption to a minimum.
- **Practice, practice, practice:** As with anything else, you will become better at video interviews if you practice with someone.

The bulk of my coaching is done on Skype for this and all the above reasons. I want my clients and you to be comfortable and prepared for video interviews. Above all, relax. If you're experiencing a video interview, you're one step closer to getting HIRED!

I met Alex Freund through a LinkedIn group we are both members of. A few of my posts got him interested in my original book and he was the first person to buy it when it launched on Amazon. We have since connected and have spoken many times. He's one of the coaches around the English-speaking world who I recommend during my workshops.

Alex Freund is known as "The Landing Expert" and for good reason. He's among the best coaches I've met. His greatest area of expertise is interview coaching and especially video interviewing (he sees clients via video as I do). His clients are always prepared for their interviews. Alex has graciously contributed some of his thoughts on video interviews.

Video Preparation

More and more job interviews are being conducted via video. Companies are under pressure to minimize talent

acquisition costs, and therefore they engage technology. Only at the very final stage, the point of decision making, are companies typically ready to assume out-of-town interview expenses (in or out of town).
Video interviewing happens in two forms. One is when a potential candidate is invited to click a link that initiates a program and is then instructed to answer a number of pre-recorded and pre-selected questions. The candidate is expected to answer the questions into the video camera, and they're usually allowed to view their recording and redo it one more time before submitting. Such a video session is then viewed by the hiring team before it makes further decisions. Companies often use such resources as taketheinterview.com, Spark Hire software, and HireVues. The second type of interview is with a live person or an entire team and may involve people located anywhere throughout the globe. Again, the technology already exists to accommodate such requirements.

Whether you're participating in the first or second type of video interview, the following guide will help you prepare. To make sure it will be a good experience for all participants, always test your PC and capabilities well in advance of the meeting.

Prerequisites to ensure a timely start in order to be respectful of all participants requires that you download Zoom, Skype, Google Hangouts, or any other video program. Test it again and again! You can't afford to be disqualified because of a technical issue with your computer or software.

General Video Tips

Following are essential steps for making sure you look your best in a video interview.

- Make sure your face is well lit, with no shadows.
- Maintain good eye contact, but don't stare.

- Smile. Smile a lot, because smiling shows comfort with the process; but make sure your smile is genuine and not forced.
- Be aware of your body movements. They are what others see.
- Avoid backlighting (e.g., bright lights or windows behind you), which will darken your face.
- Gesturing is fine as long as it's not overdone.
- Such actions as touching your face, twirling your hair, or tapping your fingers or feet are distracting.
- Avoid, if possible, using fillers like *uh-huh* or *like* too many times.
- Appear calm and collected. Practicing helps.
- Use an interview preparation coach to get feedback and suggestions for improvement.
- Sit upright and keep your back straight. Look at the camera at a 90-degree angle.
- Adjust your chair height. Too low or too high is distracting, so make sure you are centered in the camera frame.
- Avoid wearing white if possible; it appears too bright. Also avoid pure black.
- Avoid very bright colors, too, because they can make your skin appear reddish.
- Make sure that the lighting is positioned so that it does not reflect in the lenses of your eyeglasses.
- Avoid conducting the interview in a public place.
- Do not wear a busy pattern, because colors may continually shift or iridesce and be distracting.
- Softer colors are best. Dark or deep blue is usually great on camera.
- Avoid high-contrast colors.

A final thought: remember, practice makes perfect.

Note: Both Skype and Zoom have packages that allow you to record then play back your mock video interviews. Both Alex and I recommend their use.

Interview "Thrival" Tactics

There are some rules-of-thumb to keep in mind about face-to-face interviews. If some seem like common sense, it's because they are. If you do the following, you will not only survive, but thrive:

- Relax
- Smile
- Firm handshake (If you are hyperhidrotic, casually wipe your hands on your clothing. No "Dead Fish")
- Eye contact and lots of it!
- Present your business card (try to get theirs)
- Wear appropriate attire (see: Attire to Hire below)
- Sit slightly forward in your chair, never all the way back
- Use a portfolio for notes (and your "cheat sheet)
- Have a list of questions
    - Take LOTS of notes
    - Create a list of words that will remind you of the anticipated question answers, STAR, Red Flag and RATS Stories
- If you carry a briefcase, have it organized and open to be able to quickly reach for necessary documents, computer, or tablet.
- Leave your cell phone in your car or turn it off prior to arrival at the meeting place.
- Don't glance at your watch (take it off).
- Have Thank You cards with you (leave one THAT DAY!).
- Send an electronic thank-you after business hours the same day.
- Exude confidence! You're better than the other candidates, right? Show it!
- Be nice to the receptionist, people often ask them how you acted, reacted, and treated them.

- Arrive a minimum of 10 minutes early.
- Review material if you have time; don't fidget.
- Silent meditation, deep breathing, or prayer can help settle the nerves.

There's one last set of thrival tactics I found as an activity broadcast on LinkedIn that I wanted to share:

10 Things that Require Zero Talent

1. Being on time
2. Good work ethic
3. Showing effort
4. Positive body language
5. High energy level
6. Positive attitude
7. Passion
8. Being coachable
9. Doing extra
10. Being prepared

How many people (including you?) miss the mark on one or more of the above? Those who can honestly say they are at 100% (and can give examples or, better yet, have people who will tell your future boss that you possess these traits) will separate themselves from the herd.

Initial Face-to-Face Interviews

You're already pretty much prepared for interviewing;

- You have the qualifications: you were among the few of the original applicants chosen to be called, you passed the phone screening, and you are at the face-to-face. How many aren't?
- You have your stories prepared.
- You have the "thrivall tactics."
- You have practiced and honed your skills using mock video interviews.

Now it's time to look at interviewing from the Hiring Manager's point of view and it's not what you might expect. Remember, Hiring Managers don't like the interview process any more than you. They have a job that they are being judged against, and the interviewing takes time away from those duties. Also, there are a lot of things that can happen with a new hire, and few of them are beneficial to the manager's career.

Hiring Managers don't care if you need a job. S/he only cares about HIS/HER job. Here are just a few concerns:

- Will the new hire work out?
- Will the new hire stay?
- Will the new hire make her look good or bad?
- Will the new hire be a risk or reward to her career?

I'm not exaggerating when I say one bad hire can cost the manager her job. So, you're seen as a risk. Your task is to mitigate that risk and make him/her believe that it is to his/her advantage to hire you over the other candidates.

If you focus your attention on the Hiring Manager's needs, you'll have a better chance of getting what you're after. You do this by asking questions to find out what the Hiring Manager's needs and pain points are. What headaches does s/he have that you can be the aspirin for? Additional examples:

- What are the top 5-7 things I should focus my attention on after I start?
- Based on what you've shared with me today about your needs from me in this position, may I put together a short presentation for our next interview?
- What traits do your best ________(title) have in common?
- What's the company's biggest challenges in the upcoming year, and how will I be able to help overcome them in this role?

Candidates often make the mistake of leading with their resume. Few Hiring Managers have had interview training, and have spent almost no time reviewing your resume. S/he has many other candidates to consider and probably can't remember which person you are. For this reason, if you hand him/her a Chronological resume at the beginning of the interview, s/he will typically begin reading it and you've lost him/her. This is the main reason I recommend a Hybrid resume.

You want to get the Hiring Manager engaged in a conversation. This is when I recommend asking the same question you asked in the phone interview, "Hopefully, you've had a chance to review my credentials. What is it about my background that made you want to meet with me?" With my clients, very often the interview is ending before the interviewer realizes that he doesn't have your resume yet. That's a winner!

If you do hand over your resume up-front, be certain you point out its formatting; that it features what you bring to the table, with lots of examples of what you accomplished. And s/he doesn't have to dig through paragraph after paragraph to find your strengths.

> I was once challenged by a client about the usefulness of a Hybrid resume, so I applied for a few jobs, networked into the companies, and got face-to-face interviews with two of the three companies. I started one of the interviews by saying, "I hope you don't mind, but I reformatted my resume so you could quickly find some key things I can do for you rather than have you wade through a couple of pages of text." He looked at it thoroughly (me in total silence), then said, "I've never seen a resume like this before. I love it."
>
> A client asked her interviewer, "What is it that you liked best about me and what prompted you to interview me?"

> The reply was, "I loved that you had your accomplishments right up front on your resume."

This is a good time to share your Marketing Brochure or Value Proposition with the Hiring Manager. These immediately establish what you bring to the table. Include the Hiring Authority's name and the company logo in the brochure. It can get their attention. No one will have done any of this! Here's an example:

> *"Based on the job description and my initial conversation during my phone interview, I put together a short Value Proposition deck which showcases some of the things I bring to the table as a fit for this position. If we have a couple moments, I'd love share some of its highlights."*

By doing this, you have an opportunity to guide your interviewer to where you want to go. There should be give and take here as opposed to a constant barrage of questions. This will increase your confidence level and allow you to present your STAR stories.

Exude excitement about the position. Answer questions beginning with your bridging statements (planned spontaneity). Your excitement will be shared by the Hiring Manager—and excitement sells!

Many job descriptions are written by people who know nothing about the workings of the position. For that reason, I recommend asking about this possibility.

- Are there any things not mentioned in the job description I will need to focus on?
- Is there anything we haven't discussed that we should address?
- It's been my experience that Hiring Managers don't always get to write the job descriptions, so some key

elements of what the job *really* requires are missing. Are there important things we should discuss about what I should work on after I start?

Ask what you should focus on in the first 30, 60, and 90 days after you begin. Write the responses. You may want to read them back to confirm. Then ask permission to put a brief presentation together for your next interview. (You will add a 90- or 100-Day Plan to your Value Proposition deck and possibly other material).

Try NOT to explain the form of your presentation since any "pet candidates" (internal candidates) could be forewarned and one-up you, "I'd just like to make *a short presentation."* You may ask if s/he would prefer it to be on paper or on your tablet/notebook. (If you make an e-presentation, print a paper version to leave behind.)

Take note of where you're being interviewed. Is it in someone's office or in a general meeting room? If in the Hiring Manager's office, you should be aware of your surroundings. Do the walls or desk offer insight into the Hiring Authority's personality or interests? They WANT you to notice these things, even though they might not be conscious of it. This is them on a human level. Research! Find out as much as you can about them, and be sure to let your personality come through. I had a client whose research was so extensive that he greeted each of his interviewers by name and complimented each on a part of their background. He totally blew away his competition.

If humor is a part of your personality, use it - if the opportunity arises.

My favorite interview was in a then new, 5-Star hotel in New Orleans. When I arrived, I called the Hiring Manager, who told me what suite number he was in. I went upstairs and knocked on the door. He opened the door and jokingly said that if I had known that the brass thing in the middle of the door was a doorbell, I would have gotten the job without interviewing. Me being me, I said excuse me, slammed the door in his face, then beat the hell out of the doorbell. I could hear Mike laughing through the door. When he opened it, he said, "No, no, no, it's too late. You have to go through the interview."

The ice was broken.

The view from his room was amazing. You could almost touch the bridges spanning the Mississippi River. The room overlooked the French Quarter and Jackson Square. We got along so well he broke a company rule. He said he had something to show me then led me to the restroom where there was a bidet. Mike stepped on the peddle and water shot into the air. Me being me, I said in my best southern redneck accent, "Hot damn! They even got their-self a water fountain in the bathroom!"

Interviews are a bit like first dates. Be yourself! You're about to begin a relationship that may last many years. You don't want to "tie the knot" with the wrong person.

You will almost certainly be asked if you have any (other) questions at the end of the interview. Don't let this opportunity pass without a question. Here's one of the final questions I like best:

"I am really excited to begin working with you. I can see myself thriving here and being an asset to you and the company. How well do you see me as a fit?"

This is another attempt to uncover any hidden objections. You might even joke that you can make his/her life easier if you were offered the job right now—no need to waste time interviewing others. (You can get away with this if you say it with a smile on your face).

Ask for the job a minimum of three times during your interview. It's more important now than during phone interviews since the person you're speaking with is likely the decision-maker.

> *Would you prefer me to start Monday or would Tuesday be better?* (Again, said with a smile)

Note: Never smoke or have cocktails during an interview even if the interviewer does. No talk about religion or politics either. Always taste your food *before* you add any salt or pepper (I knew someone who would not hire a candidate for committing those sins - seriously!).

The Dreaded Panel Interview

It seems as if the business world has fallen in love with Panel Interviews. Now, when I talk about Panel Interviews, I lump both the type where you meet with several people during the day individually and the Firing Squad type panel where you meet with several people at the same time. Both serve the purpose to cover everyone's rear end with the thinking, "no one person can foot all the blame if everyone agrees on a candidate."

The interviewers will be from any area of the company and none of them wants to be there. These interviews are taking them away from the job they're paid to do. No matter in which type you find yourself, treat each person as an individual.

Panel interviews usually follow a script of sorts. The members are likely to pose questions or offer scenarios to test how you might react to certain situations. Take your time and use your STAR stories as examples whenever possible.

They'll also test your grasps of THEIR area of expertise. A person from accounting would be interested in your "fiscal fitness;" the person from HR wants to see if you fit the company's culture, while your future boss will question you on the job itself and how well you can do it.

Focus on the needs of the interviewer(s), it will help them want to add you to the team. You should be asking questions about like, "What can I do in my position to make your life easier?" If you can adapt a STAR story as an example of how you have done it in the past, all the better.

> Years ago, I had a client who I dubbed "The Panel Interview King." His first Panel Interview was an all-day affair, meeting twelve people in total. Even worse, it was with one of the companies he DID NOT want to work for! Sure enough, he was offered the job. I advised him to turn it down (he got a better job offer a few weeks later). A couple of years later, he became a client again. This time he outdid himself. He had a 14-person panel! Happy to say, he's once again my favorite kind of client: a former (successful) client.

No matter the form, try to get the business card of your interviewers. If the interview is around a table, place each person's business card in a way that represents where they're sitting. If you cannot, write each person's name oriented to where they are sitting. Additionally, be sure to make a note of something each person says. You can use these phrases in your personalized thank you notes. And boy, can this tactic ever help to win them over!

Most of all, relax. You can get through Panel Interviews, I promise.

Placating the Pachyderm

(The Elephant in the Room)

Have you ever been in an interview and you got the feeling something was wrong, like there was an *Elephant in the Room*?

If you get that feeling, it's probably for a good reason. Chances are, your interviewer has an objection s/he's hiding, a Hidden Objection. You can't ignore the elephant in the room. If you don't uncover and address the hidden objection, you're toast.

How do I uncover a hidden objection?

You must ask questions, open-ended, probing questions. Examples include:

"I see myself as becoming a huge asset in this position. How well do you see me as fitting?"

"When I read the job description, I said to myself, this was written with my name on it! Is there anything we haven't touched on that will be important to my success?"

"I can't wait to get started! What, if anything, might keep you from choosing me?"

"My hope is that you're seeing me as becoming your best employee. What, if any, concerns do you have that we can clear up?"

People of all ages can ask the above questions in an attempt to uncover hidden objections, but there are generational challenges (age biases) against both younger candidates and older candidates.

For years, I have led the "Baby Boomer and Older Gen-X Job Search Strategies" workshop at one of the venues where I volunteer, so you might not see me as the person who was asked to create a workshop to address the challenges of recent college graduates through younger Gen-Xers. I was, and I did.

Ironically, at that very time, I had been researching job search challenges for that age group! (If you make yourself aware of the biases against your age group, you can devise a strategy to combat those prejudices). Let's start with the younger candidates.

"Baby" Elephants (Overcoming Youth Bias)

Gen-Y & Younger Gen-X: Perceptions & Strategies

Believe it or not, you're perceived by Hiring Authorities as the "Me, Me, Me Generation." It doesn't matter one bit if you are the most selfless person on the planet, people's perceptions are the reality they live by. Life's tough so you have to be tougher.

Your job is to change their preconceived view, your fellow age group be damned! If you want a job, you have to play the game. They own the ball. If you want to play, you're the one who has to adapt. Worry about changing the rules for when you're on the inside (getting a paycheck) and own the ball.

To combat this perception, be certain to include volunteer activity you have been a part of on your resume, online profiles, and marketing material. Spend a little time pointing these things out to your interviewer. Because I'm a somewhat aggressive individual, I would tend to be proactive in my approach to this and other negative biases. My suggestion is to say something like:

"In addition to my studies (or work), I have always tried to find the time to give back to my community. Not only is it appreciated by those I help, but it also allows me to learn others' perspectives."

Based on Daniel Goleman's bestselling book, *Emotional Intelligence: Why It Can Matter More Than IQ,*[53] Younger people are perceived as lacking:

- Self-Awareness
- Self-Regulation
- Internal Motivation
- Empathy
- Social Skills

If these are their perceptions (they often are), you need to devise a strategy to show you are different from others in your age group and possess the Hiring Manager's preferred qualities. Let's revisit and plan:

Lacking Self-Awareness: You need to practice being able to identify moods, emotions and their effects on others. You can display these traits by displaying:

- **Confidence** - make eye contact, nod, and smile;
- **Realism** - Study the job's requirements and show you are willing to prove yourself at that position prior to asking for more:
- **Self-deprecating humor** - Don't take yourself so seriously. Poke fun at yourself. Show you can take a joke;

Lacking Self-Regulation: Show that you are in control of your emotions and won't run off in a snit when things don't go your way. Show these through examples of how you:

- **Think before acting -** When asked a question, pause before answering and give examples of how others rushed into something whereas you took a bit of time to think things through first.

---

[53] Daniel Goleman, *Emotional Intelligence: Why it Can Matter More than IQ*, Bantam Books, 1995.

Lacking Level-Headedness: If you have an example of an emergency, you can talk about being the voice of calm and reason.

- **Embrace change** - Others may want to maintain the status quo, whereas you have a good risk-reward ratio. Looking at the situation logically, if adopting change is the wise move, you're all in.

Lacking Internal Motivation: Hiring Managers want to know you have drive, are more than money-motivated, and can be counted on to understand and get done what's required and get it done without being under the constant eye of a babysitter.

- **Intellectual curiosity** - Ask questions about things you don't understand fully and don't be afraid of being seen as dumb. The adage, *there's no stupid questions* applies here;

Lacking Empathy: Companies want workers who can empathize with their fellow workers and are in tune with how outside influences can affect other's emotions. Show you:

- **Care** - Have you dealt with someone physically or emotionally sick or dying? Craft a story about how you were there for the person (animal).
- **Volunteerism** - As stated earlier, volunteering your time and effort speaks to your character.

Devoid of Social Skills: The people you will report to need to know you can "play nice in the sandbox" and get along with your coworkers and can be managed. Give examples of:

- **Rapport** - Give examples of how you can build rapport with others.
- **Teams** - Share stories of groups or teams you have worked on including projects at school. Scouting and team sports (including intramural) are good examples
- **Long-term relationships** - We live in a Twitter world. If you can give examples of relationships that have stood

the test of time, including your parent's friend who has known you for years and who recommended you.

Working Strategies writer, Amy Lindgren, offers seven ways to stand out after you have a job, but they can be adapted to help you land a job:[54]

1. **Focus on your boss** - If you have read anything multiple times in this book, it's that this process is all about them and never about you. Focus on the needs of the Hiring Manager and you have a better chance of getting HIRED!
2. **Help your team operate better** - If you can share, have examples (stories) of how you can and have worked with fellow team members toward achieving a goal, you are well on your way to your next job.
3. **Be reliable** - Reliability is one of many things your older compatriots believe you're lacking in. Share stories of how you can always be counted on.
4. **Own something** - Show you can (and do) go the extra mile and will do more than what you're assigned. Volunteering for tasks in addition to your duties will separate you from many others.
5. **Be solutions oriented** - Share times of when you saw a challenge and then presented solutions to that challenge. You don't want to be among the group who is good at saying something's screwy, then lays an additional problem in your boss's lap.
6. **Learn to be big picture** - Ask questions about your company's future and ask your Hiring Manager where s/he their own future is and what you can do from your position to help him/her succeed.
7. **Be cheerful** - Older workers see many of your generation as introverted, self-centered, and sullen.

[54] Amy Lindgren, How Gen Y can stand out, Pioneer Press (St. Paul, MN) Oct. 8, 2017.

Smiling and being attentive will separate you from most candidates of your own age.

There's a dichotomy between how younger workers see themselves versus how HR professionals perceive this age group. A staff editor at Beyond.com created an infographic of their different *realities.* I have turned the findings into the chart below:[55]

Gen-Y (Gen-X) see themselves	Topic Discussed	HR Professional Perceptions
65%	People Savvy	14%
35%	Tech Savvy	86%
82%	Employer Loyalty	1%
14%	Fun Loving	39%
86%	Hard Working	11%

The key here is to play up the positive perceptions of your generation while giving examples of how you have the desired qualities Hiring Managers don't believe you possess. Many are addressed above or can be adapted. Prepare stories of how you:

1. have built rapport and work well with others, both one-on-one and on teams;
2. enjoy the camaraderie of sports and how it has helped you become more well-rounded when dealing with people;

[55] Staff Editor in Human Resources, Infographic Shows What HR Pros Think of Millennials, Beyond, June 12, 2013.

3. are the sort of person who wants to see a job through completion;
4. are someone people can count on; and you
5. are willing to get your hands dirty.

I was asked to counsel a recent college graduate who was frustrated with the slow pace of her job search. We sat at a coffee shop and I listened to what her struggles were, including how fellow graduates with less experience and lower GPAs had attained employment while she was still living at home.

With a deep sigh, she was done and looked down. I said, "Let me pretend I'm you and you pretend you're a Hiring Manager in an interview. When done tell me if what I said is accurate or off the mark."

> *Do you see the same lack of work ethic from most people of my generation as I do?*
>
> *I have worked steadily since I was thirteen. I worked throughout my college years to pay for much of the tuition for my international business and marketing degree as well as all my spending money.*
>
> *One of my jobs was an internship in Spain during my junior year; I was fully immersed in the company's marketing efforts and culture. In another position, I was on a team that created the marketing material that was included in our World Cup packages. Of all the people in my age group, I know no one who is as willing to get their hands dirty as me.*

Would you hire her? I sure as heck would! (and Google did).

Show enthusiasm. No one wants to hire Eeyore! Let them know you want the job or else they will assume you don't. Engage with the Hiring Authority with a firm handshake and eye contact.

> I had three relatives use me as a coach for upcoming interviews. Two were sisters; the other was their cousin. The girls were bright, engaging, full of energy, and with smiles that could light up a room. I knew without a second thought they would be hired (healthcare field). They were.
>
> Their cousin rarely made eye contact, had a dead fish handshake, spoke down into his lap, and I doubt he could even spell smile, much less crack one. I knew he wouldn't be hired. He wasn't.

You can get HIRED! too, if you feed the elephant a few peanuts. Engage your audience. Prepare some stories to showcase what you bring to the table ... how your upbringing and education has brought you this far, and now you seek the opportunity to become a part of their team.

Tuskus Elongatus (Those Long in the Tooth)

Baby Boomer Gen-X: Perceptions & Strategies

Sorry, but I loved the Road Runner cartoons when I was a kid. When I became a father, as I was watching the same cartoons as an adult with my daughter, I appreciated the jokes' subtleties even more. At the beginning of the cartoon, the scene would stop for both creatures stating their "binomial nomenclature." The roadrunner might be *"Hotrodacus Supersonicus"* while the coyote might be *"Eatabus Anythingus."* I would laugh out loud while my daughter would look at me in disbelief. Thirty-some years later, she still does.

The previous decade has taken its toll on all of us, but maybe on no group more than Baby Boomers and upper half of the Gen-X generation. Although workers in their forties through their sixties tend to be the last to lose their jobs, they're also the last to be rehired. When they are, they can expect to be paid considerably less than what they had been making previously (upwards of 23% less)[56].

In her *The Guardian* article, Katie Allen wrote, "Older workers are worst hit when it comes to long-term unemployment, and experts warn it is a trend that will cost the economy."[57] In addition, ageism against older workers is not only rampant, it's blatant. The *Atlanta Journal-Constitution*'s Michael E. Kanell quoted the Vice President for an Atlanta area technology consulting company as saying, "We're hiring lots of **young**, vibrant, hungry, capable analysts."[58]

You may not even be able to see ads if you're above a certain age. As Monica Torres writes in Ladders, ProPublica and *The New York Times* found that dozens of top employers (Amazon, Verizon, Goldman Sachs, UPS, and Facebook to name only a few), are using Facebook, Google, and LinkedIn to create recruitment ads that target only younger job seekers. A HubSpot ad, for example, explicitly aimed at people aged 27 to 40 appeared on Facebook. The limited age range meant that people outside of those ranges would not see the ad on Facebook.[59] (thanks Gerry Lopez)

The *Kansas City Star*'s, Diane Stafford, stated that one in four members of the U.S. workforce is 55+, but with so many sidelined, "Institutional Memory" (how the business of business is conducted) may not be passed to the next generation. She

---

[56] Kimberly Foss, Don't Let a Job Loss Harm Your Retirement, Forbes, Oct. 27, 2014.

[57] Katie Allen, Ageism is Back as Unemployed over-50's Struggle to Get Back into Work, *The Guardian*, Apr. 14, 2012.

[58] Michael E. Kanell, Metro Jobless Rate Slides on Hiring Push, *The Atlanta Journal-Constitution,* Nov. 27, 2015.

[59] Monica Torres, Report: Major Companies excluding older workers from job ads on Facebook, Google and LinkedIn, Ladders, Dec. 21, 2017

also quotes a SHRM (Hiring Managers) survey stating some the advantages of hiring older workers as having:[60]

- More experience;
- More expertise;
- More maturity and professionalism;
- A stronger work ethic;
- Can serve as mentors (that institutional memory thing); and are
- More reliable.

Yet, half the organizations surveyed DO NOT recruit older workers!

It's your job as a candidate to make known the positives of hiring you versus the potential negatives of hiring someone younger. You should highlight the fact that, as opposed to young candidates, your set of attributes include:

- Loyalty to your employers;
- More productive (you come to work to work);
- Great work ethic;
- Require less training (hit the ground running);
- Require less supervision (no babysitting for you);
- Understand corporate politics (avoid potential landmines);
- Can be used as a mentor;
- No children at home (fewer trips to the doctor or school);
- No maternity leave (if my wife got pregnant, it would be the "immaculate contraception"); and
- A track record of success

In short, hiring you decreases the Hiring Manager's chance of making a bad hire. Don't be afraid to point a few of these distinctions out to your interviewers.

---

[60] Diane Stafford, Boomers' Retirement Will Hit Hard, and Many Businesses say they Aren't Prepared, *Kansas City Star*, Jan. 19, 2015.

In one of his *The Guardian* articles, Robin McCay Bell shared a series of biases against older workers. I'll address them and a few more typical objections you may encounter either overtly or covertly. Older workers:[61]

Won't work for a younger manager or with a younger team

Possible answer:

- *I've successfully worked for managers younger and older than me. My experience has been that the entire team is better when there is a mix of ideas. I can't wait to start working for you!*
- *I've worked on teams with people of different ages, genders, and ethnicities and our results have won awards. I feed off the energy of diverse groups. Don't you?*

Lack energy

Possible answer:

- Sit forward in your chair (never sit against the back of your chair)
- Show some enthusiasm!
- Smile and nod your head while the interviewer is speaking
- *I can't wait to get started and work with you closely*

Have health problems

Possible answer:

- Don't mention anything about a health issue. If it doesn't have to be said, don't say it!
- *I can't remember the last time I took a sick day*

---

[61] Robin McKay Bell, Finding Work, A Guide for the Over-40's, *The Guardian,* Apr. 29, 2011.

Are not mentally agile

Possible answer:

- *Just the other day I blogged (tweeted or commented) on that very subject. I had many very interesting responses. It got reposted by several connections.*
- *I found a great article about that by______. Would you like for me to send a bitlink of it to you?*

Can't deal with change

Possible answer:

- *One of the few things you can count on in life is change. I don't understand people who can't deal with change or are afraid of new technology.*
- *During my next interview, may I make a brief presentation on my tablet?*

Wants or will take their job

Possible answer:

- *If I'm anywhere near as good as my resume states I am, and my recommendations will tell you I am, I'm going to make your team perform even better than it does now. Hopefully, that will hasten your next promotion and if you're the type person I feel you are, you'll want to take the people who helped you along with you.*

Will get bored and leave

Possible answer:

- *I hope you can believe me when I tell you that I hate having my time wasted and I refuse to waste other people's time. If I wasn't excited about this position, I wouldn't be wasting either your time or mine. I'm here for the long haul.*

Change jobs quickly

Possible answer:

- *Take a look at my history. I've never been a job-hopper and don't plan to start now!*

Will command a higher salary

Possible answer:

- *Sure, it costs a bit more to get someone with my background, but I bet you don't want to go through the hiring process again any time soon. Unlike someone green, I'm not always jumping after every shiny new penny. I'll be worth your investment*

Are over qualified

Possible answer:

- *I would like to share my qualifications with YOUR team*
- *Yes, I am highly qualified and just as with a pilot or surgeon, I bet you would rather have someone who can get the job done right the first time and every time, someone you can always count on, someone like me.*
- *I've fought many battles in my career. Let me and my experience hasten your rise through the ranks.*

A quick story about a former client who was told he was overqualified:

> Clients are supposed to call me after interviews to debrief. His call was quite late. The phone finally rang. When I picked-up it up, all I could hear was cackling, "I did it, I did it." Finally, I asked, "What did you do?" He responded, "When I was told I was overqualified, I did what you told me to do. I asked for my resume back, and started tearing pieces off the bottom while saying, *"If you want someone who's not qualified, I promise not to work up to my capabilities. Want me to take off some more qualifications?"*

> He went on to say the guy's jaw dropped, his eyes looked like saucers and he was speechless. When he finally spoke, he muttered, "I guess that was pretty dumb." The client told me, "It took all I could not to say, Yeah, it was stupid."

Needless to say, he didn't get the job, but he sure as hell had fun!

Final Face-to-Face

You're now among the final 3-5 people in the running for the position. It's time for your star to shine brightest!

The questions you asked in the previous interviews and the research conducted are the foundation blocks for the presentation you will make. Prepare to knock their socks off!

In your previous interview, you asked permission to make a short presentation. Let's discuss its medium first. It can be on paper in the form of a:

- Bi-fold Brochure
- Tri-fold Brochure
- Multi-fold Brochure
- Flip Chart
- Portfolio
- Infographic

You can also use electronic methods to present a PowerPoint via:

- Video
- Projector
- Laptop
- Tablet

Especially for older candidates, presenting on a tablet plants the seed that you're keeping up with the times.

The content of your presentation should be brief and concise. No "Death by PowerPoint!" Instead of words, where possible, use:

- Symbols
- Charts
- Graphs
- Logos
- Flags
- Pictures as metaphors

All of these are talking points (and methods to engage the interviewer). A quick reminder of your background is a good place to start, but quickly move to the topics discussed in your previous interview, especially those things on which your future boss wanted you to focus. This is where a 30-60-90 Day Plan of Action (POA) or 100 Plan if you include a period of preparation I call Pre-Start. This plants the seed that you will hit the ground running on day-one is highly effective.

When you reach this point of the presentation it's imperative you start with a disclaimer such as:

- *"Based on our previous meeting, I took the points you wanted me to focus on and put them into a Plan-of-Action. I'm sure we didn't touch on everything. Would you mind adding things I have overlooked, or we didn't get around to discussing last time?"* Adding an asterisk with "Subject to change as necessary by Interviewer's Name. (Now you are double covered for errors and oversight.)
- *"Based on our last meeting, here are some of the things I bring to the table for your team and how I believe I can meet or exceed those needs."*
- *"I have broken-down the things you want me to focus on into three, three-month segments so you can use*

it as a benchmark of success. I know it's ambitious, but then, I set goals higher than most people. Please add any thoughts."

- *"Based on the last time we met, I put together a possible POA to achieve the action-items you mentioned. I'm sure it's not perfect, but it's a place to start. I'd love your insight, input, and approval.*

As the interviewer gets into the meat of this, your presentation should become more of a conversation. When your Hiring Manager adds something to the mix, jot it down in your portfolio or on the presentation itself (if paper). You may want to comment something like:

- "Excellent point. I can see how that would be a benefit."
- "How do you feel it would be best for me to implement this?"
- "I wondered about that and was planning to ask about its inclusion."
- "I have a hard copy for you. If you think about anything else, please ping me so I can add it to the roadmap."

Can you see how getting input from your interviewer would indicate buy-in? Besides, the more they talk the smarter you become!

Asking for input will also prove you're not trying to run the show (unless that's what the position calls for). Make it clear these points were the needs stated by the interviewer and that you're offering possible ways to accomplish those goals in a timely manner.

These are aggressive positioning statements and I'll bet the Hiring Manager will have never seen a presentation like this, nor will other candidates come close.

Differentiate yourself from the other candidates!

Finally, I have long recommended people try getting the last interview of all the candidates. Being last or next to last makes your impression linger. Remember, the Hiring Manager has spoken to 2-4 other people over a period of days. A leave-behind is great way to make another positive impression, but it's my belief (from experience) that, "the person seen last is remembered best."

WoW! Interview™

Jay Litton leads the largest church-based job networking group in the country. We have had more than 450 job seekers on campus more than once. It has been featured in multiple national network news features and is still something of a well-kept secret.

I met Jay way back when I began volunteering at Roswell Job Networking.

In addition to this enormous volunteer undertaking, Jay is a sales executive in the tech world. He has also created an interview methodology called "The WoW! Interview™." (I wish I could steal that name!). Jay has kindly agreed to add a few of his insights into how to make interviewers say, "WOW!" the next time you have a final interview.

> **D**id you know that most hiring managers don't like to interview for the job openings they have to fill? Hiring managers have daily responsibilities managing their department or company and interviewing six to eight candidates takes many hours that they don't really have.
>
> However, hiring managers are waiting for a candidate to "wow" them so they can go back to work. Unfortunately, most candidates are not focused on wowing the hiring

manager. They are focused on showing up for a traditional job interview.

I like to help job seekers get the job they want. My template for wowing the Hiring Manager and getting the offer is something I call PPQ. The candidate that is PPQ is the one that generates excitement for the Hiring Manager, so they want to hire you. According to a couple of the largest outplacement companies, hiring managers are interviewing eight candidates for a single opening. That gives you a 12% chance. A few years ago, I tracked 100 candidates that were trained on PPQ over a period of four months and I learned that they generated the job offer 46.6% of the time. Are you ready for that type of success?

PPQ stands for being the most

- Prepared,
- Passionate and
- Qualified candidate.

As a hiring manager, I have interviewed candidates that were very prepared, but they did not show enough passion. That caused me to not ask them back for a second interview with my boss. I have also interviewed candidates that were very passionate in wanting the job, but they did a poor job in preparing for the interview. I didn't hire them either. Being a qualified candidate means that you have the skills or the ability to learn how to do the job in the timetable the employer has available.

The PPQ candidate will cause the hiring manager to say "wow" or "very impressive" at the end of your interview ... many times out loud. Being able to demonstrate that you are the PPQ candidate is key to interview success. Why just show up and wing it?

In order to leverage being PPQ it is important that you know that traditional job interviews are typically divided up into three sections. In the first section the hiring manager maintains control and asks you questions, the second section the hiring manager will provide you details about the job. The third section is where the hiring manager, as a courtesy for you coming in, will ask if you have any questions. Sound familiar? In order to "wow" the hiring manager I believe you need to take a non-traditional approach and demonstrate you are PPQ.

Let's focus on the third section of the interview. This is where the hiring manager gives the candidate control and asks if you have any questions. I recommend that you delay asking questions at that moment. Instead ask permission to demonstrate how you will make a positive contribution if you are hired. This is done by typing up three of your ideas on paper in advance of the interview or using a whiteboard to share your ideas. You can expand this discussion to include industry trends or why their company is uniquely positioned for success. Is this risky? Not if you are PPQ. There is no way hiring managers expect you to know everything about the job or their company so admit this when introducing your printout or when approaching the whiteboard. It allows you to stay humble.

Are you ready to get job offers almost 50% of the time? Leveraging PPQ for your next interview can make that happen.

Twelve percent chance of getting a job offer versus almost 50% chance, which should you choose? Have we convinced you on the reasons to prepare a presentation of some sort to showcase what the Hiring Manager can expect from hiring you? If, during an interview, you show that you're the most prepared, passionate and qualified candidate, they can anticipate the same on a day-to-day basis after you're on the job.

Wow!

Exactly.

Insider Addition (Internal Candidates)

The single most difficult obstacle to overcome in all of interviewing is the Internal Candidate. As such, you must address this, the rogue elephant.

If you were ever told, "We really liked you, but you finished second," more likely than not, you fell victim to an internal candidate. You probably never even had a shot; it was the other person's job to lose from the start. Still, you have to try to pry the job away from the insider.

You can probably understand why companies would prefer hiring from within. Here are a few:

- Hiring someone from outside the company is a negative motivator for both the internal candidate passed over and the company as a whole.

  "If I'm not good enough for that job, maybe I should find a company where I will be appreciated!"

  "I can't believe management couldn't find one person from within to take over that job."

- The internal candidate is known, warts and all.
- You are a possible threat to the Hiring Manager. What if you're a bust?

It's difficult to supplant internal candidates, but it can be done, and you must make the attempt. The first step is to ask:

Are you considering any internal candidates for this position? (you MUST ask this question during the final interview)

I certainly understand why the first instinct for many Hiring Managers is to go with the internal person, but sometimes there are advantages to hire the outsider such as fresh ideas without the bias of "This is the way we've always done it."

I remember a term I learned in a marketing class I took in college. Do you remember "Groupthink?" It's when people are together a while, they start thinking alike. While that's not necessarily bad, I promise I will look at things without preconceived conclusions.

Does this always work?

No. It only works a small percentage of the time, but it's better than sitting in the garden and eating worms. I like my chances of hitting a target, if I fire the gun.

Why'd they ask THAT Question?

- *If you were a color, what color would it be?*
- *On any given day, how many cocktail umbrellas are in circulation in the United States?*
- *Would you rather be a cat or a dog?*
- *How many golf balls fit in a school bus?*

Over the last few years, asking crazy interview questions like these has come into vogue. The theory behind asking this type question was to see how a candidate would think on his/her feet; shake things up when the interviewer thought the candidate was giving cliché or insincere answers; and sometimes the interviewer just wanted to feel superior (a jerk). Hopefully, this stupidity is coming to an end.

Google was the lead actor in this movement and infamous for asking crazy interview questions. The last of the questions above is a question actually asked by Google interviewers. Thankfully, brain-teaser questions have been proven to be less effective than traditionally asked recruiting questions. In fact, they can backfire on a company's ability to recruit talent and sour individuals on the company as a whole.[62]

> Early in my coaching career, a client had been flown to a company's Los Angeles headquarters, established great rapport with the executives, and felt he had aced his interview, until the last question, that is. Then the interviewer asked, "How many cocktail umbrellas are sold worldwide on a daily basis?" He was dumbfounded and stumbled badly. He didn't get the job.

I've always thought these questions were not only stupid on the face of it where nothing meaningful is learned, but they don't represent how business is conducted.

> In the polar opposite direction, I had a client who was among the final group being interviewed for a position. The company gave all the interviewees a set of five questions each would be asked. They were to prepare answers and present their case of the situation. To me, this method is vastly superior to the crazy question method because it represents a real-life set of challenges with which an employee might be faced.

In Adam Vaccaro's INC article, *The 25 Worst Crazy Interview Questions,* not only does he share why these questions don't work, he also states that even Google has come to the realization that they didn't accomplish the company's goals. A

---

[62] Martha C. White, No-Brainer: 'Brainteaser' Job Interview Questions Don't Work, *Time*, Oct. 23, 2012.

Google spokesperson admitted, "We have shifted away from this type of question because candidates hate them, answers leak easily, and, most importantly, research on the connection between being able to correctly "solve" a brainteaser and future job performance and/or IQ is questionable and inconsistent."[63]

Don't go crazy worrying about being asked such questions, but be aware that both extremes exist.

Thanks for the Memories

You've made your impression, presented your credentials, asked your questions, and answered theirs. You've finished the interview (this pertains to ANY interview), but you haven't completed your work. Now it's time to write a thank you note. Did you know that 57% of candidates do NOT?[64]

Thank You Notes aren't important, are they?

A thank you note is one more way to get and keep your name (and Brand) in front of the Decision Maker(s). According to an Accounttemps survey, "59% of Recruiters said thank-you notes were "very helpful" for candidates, and 32% said it was "somewhat helpful."[65] So, let me see here, if 91% say a thank you note (not letter) is a positive and the majority of candidates can't be bothered to send one, maybe (juuust maybe) you might consider one of these things! It can make the difference between you getting the job you worked so hard to get and a person who worked just a tiny bit harder getting it.

---

[63] Adam Vaccaro, 25 Worst Crazy Interview Questions (and Why They're a Waste of Time), *INC*, 2014.

[64] Laura Decarlo, Job Interview Thank You Notes Guide, Job-Hunt blog.

[65] Kazim Ladimeji, How You Can Improve your Interview Success Rate with a Thank You Letter, Recruiter.com, Jan. 1, 2015.

According to The Ladder's job search expert, Amanda Augustine, "Many job seekers believe that the interview is over once they step out of the office, but that's simply not the case. Based on my decade-long experience in conducting interviews, I can attest firsthand that failure to follow-up can be the deciding factor in rejecting a candidate who is otherwise a great fit."[66]

A second example of when a follow-up thank you was a net positive is from Carol Galle, President and CEO of Special D Events, an event-planning firm in Royal Oak, Michigan. "I recently filled an open position for which I had two highly qualified candidates, but it was a thank-you note that made the difference," she says. "[One candidate] took the time to create a custom two-dimensional note card with our company's logo and a sincere, handwritten message of thanks. I want to hire people who genuinely want to work for my company, and it was clear from her effort that was the case."[67]

Can a Thank You Ever Hurt Your Chances?

In all my years of coaching, I have experienced only one company that frowned on receiving thank you notes. I had two clients wanting to get a job with an Atlanta-based child-products company. Both sent thank you notes as I instructed, and both were told they were "too aggressive." (If that's too aggressive, I'd love to be that company's competition. I'd wipe the floor with them! I can only assume this company makes money in spite of itself.)

EmploymentGuide.com claims a thank you note:[68]

---

[66] Lisa Quast, Job Seekers: No, The Interview Thank You Note is Not Dead, Forbes.com.

[67] Margot Carmichael Lester, Should You Send a Thank You Email After an Interview? Monster.com.

[68] EmploymentGuide.com, Why You Should Send a Thank You Letter after the Interview.

- Strengthens your rapport or connection with the interviewer(s);
- Emphasizes your interest in the position and the company;
- Shows your willingness to go the extra mile;
- Demonstrates your appreciation for the interview; and
- Proves you respect and value the interviewer's time.

Okay, I'm sold!

Every expert I've read says a thank you note should be sent within 24-48 hours of the interview. I say, Bunk! My advice is to bring a handful of thank you notes with you to the interview site (extras because you might make a mistake). After the interview is completed, sit in the waiting area or lobby to compose your note(s). Some of the content can be pre-written, but include something personal/professional about the interviewer (from your interview notes).

When done, ask the receptionist if s/he would mind getting the notes to the appropriate parties. Thank the receptionist profusely, they matter! If at a hotel, ask the person at the front desk or concierge to deliver the note(s) to the interviewer's room (here's where a small tip wouldn't hurt).

In addition to the hand-written note, send an electronic note (email) to the interviewer(s) after 5:00 PM. Other than giving you a second bite at the apple, this tactic accomplishes two things: it gives the impression that you work "after-hours" and it assures you of getting at least one thank you message to the interviewer (physical notes have been known to disappear).

Now let's hope for a job offer!

Negotiation

You've finally received the job offer, congratulations! But the work of your job search isn't finished. For the first (and last) time in this process, the scales have tipped in your favor. It's time to negotiate your compensation package.

What do you mean negotiate?

Almost never is the original offer a company's top dollar amount and now is when you need to squeeze as much juice from the fruit as you can. It's your only chance and in some cases, it's expected. There's almost always wiggle room to get a higher salary, time working remotely, when benefits start, better company car, higher hourly rate, the early onset of medical insurance coverage, travel and entertainment, temporary housing, relocation, additional vacation weeks, and most any other benefit. Although CareerBuilder estimates 18% of candidates get disqualified for salary demands considered too high, this happens almost exclusively in the early stages of the interview process.[69]

Remember your three salary figures from early on in the process? When you receive an offer, you want to move the bar closer to your pie-in-the-sky number. Ask for more. The worst they can say is no (in all my years as a Hiring Manager or as a Career Coach, I am aware of only two people who had their offers rescinded). If they say they can't go any higher, ask for an early review. You can even use your 90 or 100-day plan as the benchmark!

By the way, all subsequent raises or merit increases are based on your starting salary. Negotiating up an additional $500 per month equals $6,000 more per year and if you averaged a 5% increase every year, that original $6,000 will have jumped to

---

[69] Staff Writer, New CareerBuilder Study Reveals Nine Lessons for Job Seekers and Recruiters That May Surprise You, CareerBuilder, Oct. 17, 2013.

about $7,300 by year five. Of course, if you feel badly about it, send the difference my way.

Amy Lindgren suggests being skeptical if told, "This the top of our range." Agreeing with what I claim, "That doesn't mean that they've topped out their budget. There's more money available, but only if one asks for it."[70]

> I had a young client who wanted to work for a specific company so badly, she could practically taste it. She was offered the position, but the salary offered was only pennies above her walk-away number. She was inconsolable. I said, "Let's negotiate." She was convinced she could not. I told her to take the pay stub from her best pay period. *"I don't get a pay stub, it's direct deposit."* Take your bank statement, make a copy of it, mark everything else out except your best pay period and ask if the new company could match the salary of the old one. Within 3 minutes of doing this, she had increased her salary by 15% (that's a realistic percentage, too).

Now's your chance. Ask for more. They do NOT want to go through this entire process again. Besides, you were the person they liked best out of all the people they started with. Time for them to pony-up. As Don McLean said in a song (well, almost), *"The more they pay, the more you're worth,"* to them.

Attire to Hire

A fellow church-member once asked me to invite an image consultant to speak at one of my workshops. I thought it was a lame idea, but I gave it a shot. I couldn't believe how a room full of mature professionals were spellbound, scribbling notes, and

---

[70] Amy Lindgren, Working Strategies, *Pioneer Press* (St. Paul, MN), Oct. 27, 2013.

asking questions. I will never discount this part of job search again.

One of the job networking venues where I speak has a program of the same name as this subchapter. *Attire-to-Hire* has outfitted thousands of individuals (both men and women) with an interview-ready outfit. It's from head to toe. This is where I met Michael Q. Parker.

Michael is founder and President of Dressed To Deal, LLC which produces the Dressed Style Show. He's a featured speaker at many job networking events. Michael has shared his appearance advice across a broad spectrum of organizations, ranging from Fortune 200 to start-up companies, as well as non-profit, government, and religious institutions, and now he's agreed to share his "stylings" with you:

> **A**ccording to Careerrealism research, "33% of Hiring Managers make their decision in the first 90 seconds of an interview." Some major companies found the decision is made in as few as 15 seconds.
>
> Although it doesn't seem fair, it happens. Consider there has been an initial phone screening interview and the hiring manager has had the opportunity to review the candidate's resume and/or LinkedIn profile prior to an interview. There has been ample opportunity to assess the candidate's job skills.
>
> The next step is typically for the interviewer to "see the candidate." Let's face it; very seldom do we buy anything without seeing it first. It's no different in the hiring process.
>
> So, what is a Hiring Manager assessing in a face-to- face interview? I call it an assessment of each candidate's Professional Appearance Rating (PAR). A PAR is comprised of each person's ...

1. Clothing
2. Grooming
3. Body Condition
4. Body Language

When job qualification attributes are comparable among candidates, Hiring Managers often give ones with a higher PAR the advantage. Increase your PAR and increase your chances of being hired!

Here are my seven tips for improving a PAR and increasing the chances of being hired. (These tips are equally applicable to men and women.)

#1. Wear great fitting clothing

Styles change and if you can't afford new clothes at least take existing clothing to a tailor to ensure the best fit. Remember, not too baggy and not too tight. Not too long and not too short. And not too revealing!

It doesn't matter if you are wearing a suit, or slacks and a shirt, old or new. Correct fit and style are essential.

#2. Wear culturally appropriate clothing

Every workplace has a culture. If your clothing doesn't reflect the culture, it will be noticed. In the past, there was an "interview uniform" consisting of dark suits for both men and women. Those rules no longer apply.

It's better to ask your interview contact for the advice on interview attire. It could differ based on company and those conducting the interview.

#3. Updated eyeglass frames

Frames should be thought of much like clothing because there are current styles. Frames should be chosen based on the style best suited for face shape, size and skin tone.

#4. Sport a contemporary hairstyle

Neat, well-groomed, and current are the key attributes for interview hairstyles. Men should maintain facial hair with these same attributes in mind.

#5. Avoid perfume and cologne

Scents can be polarizing with people either loving the smell or hating it; others are allergic to scents. Job seekers shouldn't take the chance. The fragrance provided from bath soaps will suffice and run little risk of overpowering an interviewer.

#6. If overweight, wear clothing with a slimming effect

There is no perfect body! We all suffer from body imperfections. However, there is a proven "obesity bias" that penalizes overweight people. Overweight job seekers should dress using slimming effects provided by strategies such as darker colors, appropriate fit, slimming styles, etc.

#7. Exude confidence

- Employers want to hire confident people. Not arrogant, but confident! Use these strategies to exude confidence: Direct eye contact
- Confident smile. Smile but not too many teeth showing.
- Firm handshake (If hyperhidrotic, swipe your hand on your clothing prior to shaking)
- Erect stance when sitting and standing

Note: All the above material by Michael Q. Parker is the copyrighted property of Dressed to Deal, LLC, and the Dressed Style Show.

"I can count on one hand
the number of people who
wrote me a thank you letter
after having an interview, and
I gave almost all of them a job."
-Kate Reardon

Chapter 11: What Else Could I do?

"If you want to improve,
be content to be thought
foolish and stupid."
-Epictetus

Other Options

As I've stated repeatedly, my goal for this book is to share every way I know of to aid you in getting employment. Most of us go after traditional employment. Thankfully, there are other options.

Many of us dream of starting our own business. If there was ever a time for those with an entrepreneurial bent, to take the plunge, it is now. Unfortunately, what I've consistently observed is that people try to get a "real" job for months. By the time they explore establishing their own business, they have burned through too much of their severance or savings. The decision is made for them: they don't realize their dream.

Don't get me wrong, careful consideration must be taken. The cost of business purchase, establishment, upkeep, and ownership is sizeable. Business ownership has its risks and shouldn't be taken lightly, but if you want to own a business, start your exploration soon after separation from your previous position.

There are many business types available. Buying a franchise, an existing business, multi-level marketing, start from scratch storefront, and online entities are all options.

No matter the business type you want to start, if ever there was a time to get expert advice, it would be now. Seek a franchise or business broker. Get advice from people who don't have a financial incentive in your decision (brokers are paid by the franchise, not you). But don't take my word for it. There are experts out there.

Franchises

Before I met Bill Williams, I thought the only franchises out there were burger joints. Not only did Bill set me straight, he's never advised a client in favor of one. He let me know that most any enterprise can be (and has been) franchised. Here's Bill Williams:

> Fact: 72% of Americans dream of owning their own business.
>
> Fact: Only 3% pursue business ownership.
>
> Fact: Job tenure in the United States is less than 2.8 years and growing shorter.
>
> Fact: The staffing industry predicts boom times as employers turn to short-term contract staff. Employers will hire to meet business demands and cut contract staff as soon as the need decreases.
>
> Fact: If you're over 50 and in that dreaded "Career Transition Zone," your chances of landing a new position at the same level of responsibility, at the same level of compensation, without changing location or industry, are somewhere between slim and none.
>
> *"Entrepreneurship is one of the most liberating experiences you are ever likely to enjoy in life - Don't let anyone tell you that it's easy or that they can eliminate the risk for you. That's a lie!"*

-Milo Pinckney

"Most men die at 25 ... but they're not buried until they're 75" ... Ben Franklin

What holds most people back from exploring having their own business?

- **Fear** - Fear of failure, fear of change, fear of criticism, and fear of commitment.
- **Uncertainty** - Uncertainty over how to proceed, whom to believe, and how to avoid being "sold a bill-of-goods."
- **Doubt** - Doubt if you have what it takes.

We like to say that franchising is entrepreneurship for the corporate soul because most of our clients are corporate "refugees," forced into early retirement or downsized to cut costs.

In the corporate world, we are accustomed to structure, procedures, training, and organization. Franchising offers systems for managing your business, procedures to follow, and training and coaching to help the new franchise owner achieve success. You can reduce your business ownership risk by investing in a franchise.

The first step toward working for yourself is to be clear about why you want to own a business. What most people want from a business:

- More control of your life and career;
- More flexibility in your day;
- More balance between work and lifestyle;
- Greater personal and professional challenges;
- Retired, but looking to continue a productive life; or need supplemental retirement income;

- Giving back to your community or making a difference in the lives of others;
- To be your own boss;
- People really want financial freedom, which will provide all of the above.

Acquiring a franchise includes the operating systems and a proven way of doing business. This allows the franchisee to concentrate on running the business. The franchisee receives support from the franchisor and a large network of franchisees who have been where s/he are going. You know what you're getting, because of the information in the Franchise Disclosure Document, and by speaking with the existing and former franchisees whose contact information must be provided. The infrastructure is defined, a product line in place, and the marketing strategy developed. The pooled resources of many franchisees allow promotional opportunities and group buying power.

A franchise is a group of systems that can be systematically applied by any franchisee in a step-by-step method that incorporates the systems into the operation of their franchise unit. The systems create a predictable way to produce results if the franchisee is willing to give the time and attention it requires to flourish. There are over 3,000 different franchise brands in 80 different categories!

Advantages of Owning a Franchise:

- Established product or service,
- Proven systems of operations,
- Initial training / ongoing support,
- Experience of franchisor,
- Other franchisees in the system,
- Understand your customer,
- Group purchasing power (products/advertising),

- Easier to get quality locations,
- Start-up Assistance,
- Assistance in Financing – (easier to obtain),
- Name recognition,
- Vehicle for organized growth,
- Typically, experience with the product/service is not required

Axxiom and other franchise brokers provide help and guidance to people who want to own their own business(es), so they can make an informed buying decision. Axxiom has a national team of advisors who help prospective buyers develop a plan for finding the right franchise opportunity.

Your advisor will conduct an interview to develop a personal profile that outlines your personal needs, business requirements, and financial goals. The advisor will then research and identify franchise opportunities that match your unique personal profile and present them to you for your consideration.

The advisor will introduce you directly to the appropriate franchise personnel. Your Axxiom Advisor will advise and coach you throughout your due diligence and decision-making process, but the final decision is always yours to make, at no cost to you!

Existing Business Purchase

Doing something you love doing seems like a dream. Realizing a dream that already has a base of business would be even better. Purchasing an existing business could be that dream. It's certainly an option.

There are advantages to buying a "going concern." Existing businesses:

- Are already generating revenue;

- Have an existing customer base;
- Can train you directly during transition; and
- Have a model for you to follow.

On the other side of the coin, existing businesses are sold at a premium (higher than a franchise) because they are already profitable. Just as with a potential franchise purchase, it's wise to find a professional broker. Not only are they aware of more available businesses, they will help you find businesses that meet your criteria. They will help you with due diligence, terms of the deal, and obtaining financing. In short, a business broker will offer advice that can help you avoid costly mistakes.

Here are some questions you should be asking in an effort to uncover a good business broker:

- Does s/he have a network of brokers who share listings or is the person a solo act? (you want the former, not the latter.)
- How long has the person been a broker? Experience counts for a lot.
- Does the broker fully understand your personal goals and objectives? You want someone you're comfortable communicating with.

Most of all follow your gut instincts. If you don't feel the fit is right or if the broker is pushing you toward a particular property that doesn't appear right for you, go elsewhere. An existing business shouldn't run you; you should run it!

The Better Mousetrap

For those of us who have had an idea and/or the desire to start your own business, a lot of wishing, hoping, thinking, and praying comes to mind as appropriate. For many reasons, the four words may be as far as you have taken things. Now may be the time to add acting to the mix.

Starting your own "retail" business is probably the riskiest of all business propositions. If done right, though, it can also be the most rewarding and profitable. It's the getting it right part that's so challenging. A start-up needs careful consideration, much research, a sound business plan, hard work, some luck, and enough money to sustain you until it attains profitability.

Start with your brand. Is it recognizable? Does it clearly differentiate you from other, similar companies? Your idea may seem like a unique, slam dunk to you, but do others see your idea as a clear advantage over other similar businesses? Will the buying public see the difference and be willing to buy into it?

You will have to set up:

- A Marketing Campaign,
- Financing,
- Employees, possibly including management,
- Suppliers,
- Controls and supervision over all the above

From-scratch businesses give the proprietor the ability to create a business model without having to answer to anyone. They can succeed or fail within the purview of its creator. How liberating!

Most new businesses fail, meaning the risk of starting a new business is high. There's also a lot of added pressure involved with starting a new business due to having to deal with so many unforeseen factors.

The REAL start-up cost of a new business can be surprisingly high because of the need to make people aware of your business. Another factor to consider is that most banks see independent enterprises as a higher risk to the point that a bank you have done business with for decades is apt to turn you down or require a bigger bite than you expect. There is the definite possibility that you would be charged a higher rate than if you were purchasing an existing business or a franchise.

Not to be a "Debbie Downer," but in a Forbes article, Eric T. Wagner claimed, "Eight of ten entrepreneurs who start businesses fail within 18 months."[71] But don't let this stop you! Even when considering mergers, acquisitions, and bankruptcies, the average life expectancy of a business (including publicly traded companies) is only 10 years.[72]

Once you have started your business, you have to drive customers to it. We have all heard the saying, "If you build a better mousetrap, the world will beat a path to your door," (attributed to Ralph Waldo Emerson) but how?

I wish I had a rock-solid answer to the above question. Advertising, word-of-mouth and Search Engine Optimization (SEO) are part of the equation, but only part. Both time and money are involved, but even those don't insure victory.

Don't be afraid to start your own business from scratch. Be smart and careful.

Online Entities

Without a doubt, the least risky business is an online entity. But, no matter what your online business is, making customers aware of your product or service, driving them to your website then getting them to part with their cash is the challenge, especially when there are so many other businesses on the web.

---

[71] Eric T. Wagner, Five Reasons 8 of 10 Businesses Fail, *Forbes*, Sept. 12, 2013

[72] Rishi Lyengar, How Long Will Your Company Last, according to Science, *Time*, Apr. 2, 2015.

An advantage of a virtual business is that your customer base can be worldwide. There are no borders for many products. For example, in one week's time a woman from Switzerland and a man from Sweden purchased my first book (I know because both asked to connect on LinkedIn).

Be strong and flexible. Your business can change as necessary, but beware of trying to be everything to everyone because you can become nothing to no one, as is the case in traditional job search.

Remember too, that the customer isn't always right. Sometimes it's better to walk away from business. I made a mistake typical of new business owners; I acquiesced when prompted by a partner to lower my fees. This caused me to work harder for less and it attracted a more difficult clientele. Now, I will recommend other coaches to the "bargain hunters." Don't sell yourself short; stick to your pricing structure.

Shopify created a competition among 10,000 online businesses. The top five names were: GameKlip, GoldieBlox, Fresh-Tops, Canadian Icons, and SkinnyMe Tea (all of which are still going concerns as of the date of publication). Bonnie Wertheim, in her Mashable article, shares the commonalities of these business owners:[73]

1. **Decide and Do** - If you find a problem in need of a solution, create that solution then offer it to the public.
2. **Test and Test Again** - Extensively test your product or service before making it available to the public.
3. **Ace the Manufacturing Process** - Search for local manufacturers and rapid prototype shops. Control and communication can be a greater savings than searching the world in an effort to make an extra dime.

---

[73] Bonnie Wertheim, 5 Ways to Launch a Successful Online Business, *Mashable*, Sept. 30, 2013.

4. **Find Untapped Resources** - Try up-and-coming social media to uncover mentors.
5. **Create Big PR Wins** - Look to gain high SEO, links, and mentions in respected publications to drive traffic and build brand identity.

There will be ups and downs, but enjoy your journey.

Multi-level Marketing

Another alternative to traditional jobs is multi-level marketing. It's not for everyone (certainly not me), but it could be perfect for you. Many people have been highly successful selling soap, vitamins, make-up, and Lord only knows what else.

I still see a lot of pink Cadillacs on the road, don't you?

Trade Ya!

My father, God rest his soul, had two PhDs, but didn't know the difference between a screwdriver and a hammer. Most of us are not do-it-your-selfers!

It's been drilled into our heads for decades that the only way to get ahead is to get a bachelor's degree; then it was, you gotta have a Master's if you want to separate yourself from the crowd. What with the skyrocketing cost of college, these long-held truths are finally being questioned.

According to CollegeData, the 2016-2017 average cost of an in-state college education is about $25,000 per year and the annual outlay for a moderately priced private institution is a cool fifty grand.[74] Oops, we forgot a few minor expenses like room and board, fees and services, transportation, books, and

---

[74] Collegedata, What's the Price Tag for a College Education.

supplies (not to mention beer and pizza). Talk about sticker shock!

Should you consider a career in the trades versus going the "professional" route of 4-7 years of college then starting your work life tens of thousands of dollars in debt?

The *Manchester Journal*'s William Schmink asks a series of interesting questions, "When was the last time you could get an electrician, plumber, or other skilled laborer to show up on the same day you called? Have their fees gone up or down? Why are there 200,000 or more high-paying manufacturing jobs left unfilled ...?" "Vocational or trade schools are making a comeback. Over the last five years, these schools have experienced relatively strong growth, about 4.1% annually, and are expected to continue to grow by about 2.6 percent a year over the next five years."[75]

I highly recommend anyone interested in the trades to read an article by Trent Hamm, where he compares trade school versus attaining a college (bachelor's) degree.[76] His findings are thought provoking if you have an aptitude for the trades or you aren't overly thrilled with the idea of sitting in classrooms for another four or five years, then still not knowing what you want to do with the rest of your life.

(I created the chart below from Mr. Hamm's article).

---

[75] William Schmink, Trade School vs. College, *Manchester Journal*, Mar. 28, 2013.

[76] Trent Hamm, Why you Should Consider Trade School Instead of College, *The Simple Dollar*, Oct. 19, 2017.

Bachelor		Trade School
$127,000	Cost of Study	$33, 000
$154,000	Financing 10 years at 4% interest	$40,000
$46,900	Starting Salary	$35,720
22-26	Age Starting Career	19-21
No	Job Security?	Yes
Yes	Outsourceable?	No
Yes	Greater Later Life Earnings Potential?	No

Granted, the lifetime earnings potential for those with a college degree is much greater than building a life working in the trades and the effects on one's body lean heavily in favor of the white-collar worker versus those in flannel shirts and jeans (I can attest to this personally since I have done both. Custom-made $1,500 suits are darn nice).

For many, writing a check to get work done is superior (and cheaper in the long run) to the do-it-yourself route. Who will you write the check to? It's probably to someone who has gone to trade school.

Close Enough for Government Work

Somewhere near 2 million people are employed by the United States government; it's America's top employer. Only about

10% of those employed are based in the nation's capital, the remainder work throughout the USA and abroad. Government employees are hired for just about every career field and occupation.

Almost everything about getting a government job is different from securing employment in the private sector. Resumes are different: a traditional resume is two pages (except for IT) and full of bullet points, whereas a government resume uses paragraphs and can be a dozen or more pages in length.

I have to admit, getting a government job is an area about which I have just about zero knowledge, but this is supposed to be an all-inclusive book. Your first step might be to check out USAjobs.org. It's a great general source for finding available positions within government agencies.

What if I want to work for a specific agency?

Alison Doyle suggests looking on the careers page of the agency you're most interested in because some do not post to USAjobs.org (I learn something new every day!). Whether you apply through USAjobs.org or the agency's careers page, Ms. Doyle says all submissions must contain the following:[77]

Job Information

- Announcement Number, Title and Grade(s)

Personal Information

- Full Name, Mailing Address, Zip Code, Phone Numbers (day and evening)
- Social Security Number
- Country of Citizenship - in most cases you will need to be a U.S. Citizen

---

[77] Alison Doyle, How to Find a Federal Government Job, *The Balance*, Aug. 10, 2016.

- Veterans' Preference - if you are a veteran
- Reinstatement Eligibility - if you have previously worked for the federal government
- Highest Federal civilian grade held

Education

- High School - Name, Address, Zip Code, date of diploma/GED
- College/University - Name, Address, Zip Code, Degree(s), and Major(s)
- List credits earned if you did not graduate

Work Experience

- For each job:
    - Job Title (include series and grade if Federal job)
    - Duties and Accomplishments
    - Employer's Name and Address
    - Supervisor's Name and Phone Number
    - Note whether your current supervisor can be contacted
    - Start and End Dates (Month/Year - Month/Year)
    - Hours Per Week, Salary

Other Qualifications

- Job-related training courses (give title and year)
- Job-related skills (other languages, computer software/hardware, tools, machinery, typing speed, etc.)
- Job-related certificates and licenses (current only)
- Job-related honors, awards, and special accomplishments (publications, memberships in professional/honor societies, leadership activities, public speaking, and performance awards)
- Give dates, but do not send documents unless requested.

You can certainly understand how these resumes and applications can take considerable time both to complete and read! Don’t expect a snap decision for a job with the Feds, but it can be a good career.

Stringin' Things Together

Some years ago, I coined a phrase for the people who were forced to string multiple jobs together during the Great Recession. I called these poor souls Stringers. Unfortunately, I still see many Stringers today.

What's worse is that many of those who have it easy, think Stringers brought their plight onto themselves and merely have to *pull themselves up by the bootstraps* by going back to school, getting training or, if they're not making enough, just get another part-time job.

Wouldn't it be great to live in such blissful ignorance?

Even if you could string multiple part-time jobs together and were able to work a full 60 hours per week (every week), at minimum wage, you'd barely eek out an existence slightly above the poverty line for a family of four.[78] Of course, I'm making many assumptions that are highly questionable, such as:

1. Getting and keeping a second part-time job;
2. Both employers working with the other employer's schedule;
3. Working a full 60 hours per week;
4. Seamless travel from job to job;
5. Never missing a day of work; and
6. Never getting sick or needing to take a child to the doctor (if you could afford paying for the visit) or missing for some other reason.

Once one enters the Stringer way of life, it's almost impossible to get out of the downward spiral; survival is the goal. There's

---

[78] Health and Human Services, Annual Update of the HHS Poverty Guidelines, *Federal Register*, Jan. 31 2017.

no time for self-improvement like school, certifications or training. How much time does a Stringer have to raise their children who are almost certain to follow in their parent's footsteps (or worse).

Stinging is more like a hangman's noose. The time they spend at the menial job increases while time invested toward getting a real job is relegated to the back burner. Others have gone the ride-share route, but the best fare times are the best job search times. In every case, their period of transition becomes longer than they (and I) would have otherwise expected.

I'd prefer, if at all possible, that you focus on search rather than consider a "side hustle" (I hate that term) and play financial catch-up after you settle into the new job.

WIOA

I hesitated inclusion of information on the Workforce Innovation and Opportunity Act (WIOA) because there has been consistent congressional pressure for the program's elimination (we wouldn't want to train people for better jobs, would we?).

WIOA is legislation designed to strengthen and improve the US' workforce system, help get Americans into high-quality jobs, and careers, and help employers hire and retain skilled workers.[79]

I recommend checking the website to make certain the program still exists, what restrictions are in place, any limitations, and what else is necessary to take advantage of this great program. Here are a few additional resources:

Department of Education

Office of Career, Technical and Adult Education (OCTAE): http://www.ed.gov/AEFLA

---

[79] https://www.doleta.gov/wioa/

Office of Special Education and Rehabilitative (OSERS) - Rehabilitation Services Administration:
https://rsa.ed.gov/wioa.cfm

Department of Health and Human Services
Peer TA website:
https://peerta.acf.hhs.gov/ofa-initiative/426

"If you're facing the right direction,
all you need to do is keep walking."
-Attributed to Buddha,
(actually written by
Joseph Goldstein)

Chapter 12: Parting Shots

"By failing to prepare,
you are preparing to fail"
-Benjamin Franklin

And the Horse You Rode in On

A few hundred pages ago, you were unemployed and had no idea which direction to take to get to your destination. Today, you know how the "game" is played and are employed again (or are a helluva lot closer than you were when you started reading this book). My question is: Do you want to go through this entire process again?

Hell, no I don't want to go through this again!

I hate to inform you, but you are almost certain to change jobs again. The question I asked was if you wanted to go through this *entire* process again. As a society, we average about 12 jobs during our professional lives, and that number is liable to increase. I'm glad you got a job, but you are certain to need one again in the not-so-distant future and if you don't continue applying the lessons you learned during this exercise, you will have to start from scratch again. "Those who don't learn from history are doomed to repeat it."

It's been a strange trip to get to this point. What have you learned, and will you continue to apply those lessons?

Long Strange Trip

Apologies to the Grateful Dead and Gerry Garcia, but job search is a "long, strange trip." What lessons have you learned, and will you continue working on them to minimize your next period of transition?

What have you done and learned?

- **Direction** - What direction you want to head in (formal and/or informal assessments).
- **Contacts** - You have an expanded list of contacts and know how both to build and attract connections, including Recruiters and executives.
- **Branding** - You've created a marketable Brand.
- **ATS-Formatted Resume** - You've learned how to write a resume with a cover letter that passes through Applicant Tracking System software packages, gets into the hands of Recruiters, and impresses Hiring Managers.
- **Hidden and Posted Job Markets** - You've found out where the jobs are and how to position yourself to get found for those jobs.
- **Getting Found** - You've learned how to attract Recruiters.

Unfortunately, you've also experienced what it's like to struggle through job search, but you're better for the experience – if you continue to position yourself to get found now and in the future.

How to keep them working for you:

- You beefed-up your LinkedIn profile and resume to get a job. You need to maintain a current resume on the Boards and continue adding material to stay relevant (and found).
- You set-up Google Alerts to position yourself as a resource. You need to continue re-posting industry-related articles and post your own material.
- You learned that everything moves faster these days and people become obsolete more quickly. You need to take courses, go through training classes, offer to be a

part of projects and keep your ear-to-the-ground for things new, novel, and innovative (both on the job and job search fronts).
- You learned that people who are active on LinkedIn get found considerably more often. You should set aside a couple hours every week to comment on and post articles to LinkedIn.

A Contract for Your Future

During one of my small-group coaching calls, a recent client told me of a company she was interested in going to work for. I immediately went to LinkedIn to see who I was connected to at that company. Bam! I was connected to a former client. What a break, I thought. I reached out to the former client to initiate contact between the two.

The former client didn't have an easy go of it during her period of transition, so it would be safe to assume she would bend over backwards for me, right? To my surprise, she did nothing more than agree to meet over the phone for a few minutes. There was little insight into the company offered, no desire to connect, and no offer to either look-up the Hiring Authority or present the client's resume. She'd "forgotten" what it was like for her.

I can't tell you how disappointed I was.

Will you help those in transition?

- Do you remember the deafening silence from all the people you reached out to who never lifted a finger? How did they make you feel? Will you be like them or will you accept the coffee meeting when asked?
- Do you think about the people who assisted you during this period of darkness? Will you make the time to volunteer?

- How many times did you believe you were perfect for a job, but were passed-over (because you were over or under-qualified, too young/old, or had been out of a job for a while)?
- Will you be afraid that a candidate will "take your job")? Or, will you surround yourself with and be an advocate for hiring the BEST person?

Will you enter into a contract with me to end the insanity of those hiring biases that kept you from getting a job sooner than you did? You can call it a sanity clause; every contract has a sanity clause.

Hahahaha! You can't fool me, there's
no sucha thing as a Sanity Clause!

Hey, I'm the one who's supposed to tell the bad jokes!

You told bad jokes for almost 300 pages!
Now it's my turn. Besides, I learned this from you.

Well, at least there's proof you picked-up *something* from me and this book. No offense, but I hope you never need me or anyone like me again (I mean that in the best possible way). But, if you do, you can always reach out to me.

Wishing you nothing but the best,

Al Smith
"the HIRED! guy"

"Ils Sont Partis!"
(And they're off! in French)
-Gene Griffin
(Originator & Former Evangeline
Downs Track Announcer)

"Th-th-th-that's All Folks"
-Porky Pig

Acknowledgements

To write a book, one sits singularly in front of a keyboard and monitor, but it's certainly not a solitary effort. Friends and family lend moral and technical support. More of you have done so than I can possibly remember. I apologize in advance for the people I will have missed (you may have been overlooked but are not underappreciated).

I certainly appreciate all the contributors who shared their insight with me and you, the reader. I hope you will seek their talent. Contact information is in the next section.

Thanks, first, to Rev. Richard Burdick, Diane Glynn, Al Mango and the entire staff of Unity North Atlanta Church for making the facility available to me two to three times per month for all these years. The same must be said about everyone at Roswell UMC who has endured my presence even longer than UNA. Special kudos to Jay Litton, Katherine Simons, Karen Griggs, Charlie Brown, Pam Murphey (Bondye bon touton!), Roger Davis, Gordon Zimmerman, Jim Hallberg, Bob Schnackenberg, Cliff Riviere, Wally Anderson and Cedric Allen.

My personal sounding boards include Paul Abbott, Max Sutherland, Don Harris, Mike Hydzik, Phil Nickerson, John Byers, Eric West, Victor Domenech, and Lisa Sisson, to name just a few.

Carolyn Benkowitz was indispensable by volunteering to mark-up my first run-through without calling me a dummy (at least not to my face). She helped keep my embarrassment to a minimum when the manuscript went to the editor.

Thanks Mom, Shannon, Debbie, and Leslie. I love you all!

Most of all, thanks to my wife, Terry, who has endured and supported this and almost every other cockamamie idea of mine. I couldn't have achieved this effort without your support.

Recommended Resources

Michele Brant

Michele is known for her heartfelt support of her clients' goals, respect for their values, and dedication to their growth. She is a certified Professional Coach with the Institute for Professional Excellence in Coaching (iPEC) and has an International Coach Federation (ICF) aligned Professionally Certified Coach credential. She has a BS in Industrial Management, Business Marketing and Computer Science from Georgia Tech. Michele Brant, CPC, ICF Accredited, ELI-MP, Certified Executive Coach-Career, Leadership & Wellness |Training|Motivational Speaking|Virtual Coaching Leadership, Wellness, and Career Coaching

(704) 907- 6087

www.michelebrant.com

June Burchfield

June is Talent Director at KMA Talent and can be reached at her office number: (404) 781-9366,
email: june@kmatalent.com and through her
website: www.kmatalent.com

Lisa Carman

If you are looking for a career transition support professional who takes the time to talk with you individually to understand your situation and needs, Lisa carman could be your coach of choice. Be sure to check for Client Testimonials, LinkedIn Recommendations and other professional qualifications. Lisa Carman, Resume Guru and LinkedIn Profile Expert, Resonating Resumes, LLC

Email: lisa@resonatingresumesllc.com
LinkedIn: linkedin.com/in/lisacarman-resumes/
Office: 303-947-6242

Kelly Fabian

Kelly Fabian Photography:
Great Photos represent the best in your Brand!!

Photography is very often what can make or break a first impression and it is an integral part of brand recognition. A good image helps sell your "Image"! Photos, Logos, Illustration and Copy need to work together like a well-oiled creative machine.

If you care enough to invest in quality photographs for your marketing and advertising needs, it speaks volumes about how you value your brand. Whether it be a product or an organization, presenting it with high quality visuals is essential for increased sales and brand recognition.

kelly@kfabianphotography.com
(678) 429-9418

Dave Farrell

David A. Farrell is a Financial Advisor and has been providing comprehensive wealth management services to his clients for more than 20 years. David works with private clients and institutions to create an investment plan tailored to each client's unique needs.

With his deep experience and commitment to service, David develops a client profile, works to construct a long-term strategy, and implements a plan to help his clients achieve their financial objectives. Before joining Wintrust Wealth Management, David spent 13 years serving high-net-worth clients at JPMorgan Chase.

David graduated from the University of New Orleans with a Bachelor of Science degree in Economics and holds FINRA Series 7 and 66 Licenses, in addition to Illinois Life and Health

Insurance Licenses. He is also a CERTIFIED FINANCIAL PLANNER™ practitioner. He volunteers with the Park Ridge Wilderness Scouts and Princesses and lives in Park Ridge, Illinois, with his wife, Leslie, and three children.
Dave can be reached at (630) 545-4375

David Frank

David Frank graduated from the Honors Program at the University of Georgia Summa Cum Laude with Honors with a BBA in Finance. David is a Partner at Peachtree Wealth Advisors. Peachtree Wealth Advisors is an independent comprehensive financial services firm committed to helping clients improve their long-term financial goals.

Asset Management - Financial Planning - Insurance

David S. Frank, CFO
Peachtree Wealth Advisors, Inc.
300 W. Wieuca Rd. NE Suite A205
Atlanta, GA 30342
o 404 531-0965 f 404 531-0966
www.peachtreewa.com

Alex Freund

Known as "The Landing Expert," Alex Freund helps clients land positions and promotions through effective interviewing. As a former director at Honeywell, Sanofi and Tyco International, Alex has hired hundreds.

Currently, Alex is career coach with expertise in improving interviewing and making them confident and comfortable in the interviewing process. Alex has helped more than 700 clients ranging from managers to senior executives and CEOs in a multitude of industries.

Alex teaches a course for people in transition via the Princeton Adult School and publishes The Landing Expert List, a free directory of job-search networking groups via his website at landingexpert.com.

Alex is a graduate of Cornell University and speaks five languages.

Steve Graham

Steve founded The Oval Group LLC in 2003, which now serves hundreds of clients, to specialize in assessment tools that enable business owners and corporate executives to make informed strategic decisions about their unique business and the people who hold the keys to its success. "We exclusively use TTI SI tools, because in my experience, they are absolutely the best available." – One of the reasons he is certified in every tool TTISI offers. TriMetrix Assessments are available at wholesale prices through the HIRED Store on theHIREDguy.com website. You can also contact The Oval Group directly:
https://ovalgrp.com/

Tyrone Griffin

Tyrone is a long-time dinner speaker and table volunteer at Roswell UMC Job Networking and leads the Bunny Slippers Are Evil Blogcast on various topics including life transition, motivation, job search, personal financial management and investing.

Tyrone's Websites include:

TyroneGriffin.com, BunnySlippersAreEvil.com and 3DResumes.net. Tyrone can also be reached at: Tygriffin@aol.com and (678)439-9767.

Eric Handler

Eric is a partner at Handler & Associates, one of the premier retained search firms in the Southeast. The firm has been in business for over 30 years and has successfully executed over 2700 executive searches.

Eric is also founder of Career Handler which was founded as a result of his volunteering at Atlanta JobSeekers. The Career Handler system is designed to take the guesswork out of the search process and help job seekers get more out of the time they dedicate to their search.

Job seekers are encouraged to visit our website and join our community. We offer a proven system with measurable results and accountability. Learn more by registering for one of our upcoming webinars at the Career Handler website:
careerhandler.com

Jay Litton

Jay Litton has been the leader of one of the largest job networking ministries in the United States at RUMC Job Networking in Roswell, GA since 1997. Jay is the creator of the WoW! Interview™ at www.WowInterview.com which has helped thousands of people learn practical methods for winning job offers. Jay's day job is as the Southeast Sales Director for MapR Data Technologies which is a leading big data platform software company. Contact Jay at: Jay@littongroup.com

Richard Morgan

Richard is a professional branding expert, outstanding resume writer, an outplacement specialist and career coach. He has been a long-time volunteer at Roswell UMC Job Networking and is a member of theHIREDguy.com network. Richard is known for his ability to empathize with those in transition while simultaneously coax candidates to attain more than they thought possible.

Richard can be contacted through www.theHIREDguy.com

Michael Q. Parker

Michael is President of Dressed Clothing Club. He's a featured speaker at many job networking events and has shared his appearance advice across a broad spectrum of organizations ranging from Fortune 200 to start-up companies as well as non-profit, government, and religious institutions.
(www.dressed.club)

Chad Phillips

Chad Phillips Photography: We are visual Story Tellers on a mission to make a positive impact in the world...
Chad Phillips Photography
1908 W. 42nd Street ~ Sioux Falls, SD 57105
605-336-0777
photos@chadphillipsphotography.com

Kat Phillips

Kat is a freelance editor whose services can be contracted for through Upwork.com.

Cindee Sapoznik

Cindee A. Sapoznik, CLC is a Certified Life Coach, interview Guru, volunteer, advocate for at-risk teens and women and is founder of 2myPlace (a 501c3) for Teens and Young Adults.

Cindee can be reached at: one2oneteencoach@gmail.com and at 770-815-6044

Cathy Seifert, PhD

Dr. Siefert is CEO of Eastern Shore Psychological Services and has worked for 30+ years in the areas of mental health, criminal justice and addictions. Dr. Siefert specializes in the assessment and treatment of individuals at-risk for violence and who are emotionally disturbed. She lectures nationally and provides training on the topics of "Assessing the Risk of Violence," Attachment Disorders," and "Bullying." Her books include her award-winning *How Children Become Violent;* the college textbook, *Youth Violence;* the guided journal, *5 Secrets to Help Solve Problems and Relax;* and *Big B and little b bullies: 5 Proven Tips to Stop All Types of Bullying Right Now.* She testifies as an expert witness, lectures internationally, and has appeared on CNN, Discovery ID, Fox News and a variety of local TV and radio networks.

Bill Williams

Bill specializes in helping "corporate refugees" and retiring military move into franchise ownership. He works nationwide with clients to "Re-Invent Their Future" by choosing to become a franchise owner; taking charge of their future, overcoming fear, uncertainty and doubt to be their own boss; assisting career changers from the corporate and military sectors find the best business model to attain personal and professional goals.

Bill can be reached at BWilliams@4Axxiom.com and (770) 973-0878